Praise for Cheryl Koenig's work

An overwhelming personal narrative about the strength of one woman, her family, enduring love and caring. When blood ties are strong, family is key and no one more than Cheryl Koenig can show us the incredible importance of living a fulfilled life with family. The fragility of life as experienced and documented so beautifully in this book is never to be underestimated. *In My Blood* is an honest look at how one woman faced tremendous health issues, the power of fate, and how this resilient family unit has continued to care, love and laugh in spite of all they have experienced.

In My Blood is Cheryl Koenig's best read yet!

— Elena Katrakis, CEO, Carers NSW

I heard Cheryl speak at an author talk and was interested from the outset. After purchasing her book, *With Just One Suitcase*, I couldn't put it down. Was intrigued by the wonderful storyline and the hardships the characters endured both before, during and after World War 2. Then the story came close to home with their emigration to Sydney and the new life they created in their new country. Still find it hard to believe the two families were brought together thousands of miles from where the two boys (grandfathers) grew up. Great writing and well worth the read.

— *Booktopia* Review

Like so many stories of survival and escape during World War II, this tale of two Romanian families, one Jewish, the other Catholic, is gripping. The principal figures are Frici (Frederic) Löw and Istvan (Steven) König, who knew each other in their home village of Timisoara. Through a combination of bribery, quick wits and caution both children and their families survived the Germans only to face the task of fleeing the Russians. Cheryl Koenig dramatises their plights in much the same way as a novel, life in an occupied town as well as their escape making dramatic reading. Eventually they all fetch up in Australia, Istvan mesmerised by the sight of

Sydney Harbour one autumn morning in 1950. Remarkably, in Australia, the two families merged when Frici's daughter, the author, married Istvan's son, rounding the tale with an almost Shakespearean final act.

— Fairfax Review

Cheryl Koenig's account of the life challenges thrown at her reflect a unique combination of humility——she radically underestimates her contribution to her son's recovery from a catastrophic brain injury——and stoic resilience——she's one of the few who can truly claim to have "beaten" cancer. This is *the* textbook in overcoming adversity.

— Nick Rushworth, Executive Officer,
Brain Injury Australia

Cheryl Koenig OAM is a carer. Her advocacy for carers and in particular our community organisation, Sutherland Shire Carer Support Service, is as extraordinary as she is. Cheryl has donated tens of thousands of dollars to SSCSS through book launches, book sales and personal donations. I have witnessed Cheryl at deaths door yet she still finds breath to fight for the needs of carers. The most consistent words I hear from Cheryl is 'what can we do!' I am honoured to call her not only a colleague but importantly a friend. It was an honour to read her inspirational book. On behalf of carers in our community, thank you. You will never know the true impact of your work but carers you support do.

— Tracy Sami, Manager, Sutherland Shire
Carer Support Service, NSW

In 2009 Cheryl was named NSW Woman of the Year and last year she received the Medal of the Order of Australia for services to the disability sector. Reading her enthralling family memoir [*With Just One Suitcase*], it is easy to see where she has inherited her skills and her determination.

— *Toowoomba Chronicle*

 **Cheryl Koenig OAM** is a Sydney-based writer and motivational speaker. *In My Blood* is her fifth book; her previous publications are *With Just One Suitcase* (Wild Dingo Press, 2015), *Paper Cranes* (2008), *The Courage to Care* (2007) and *There's always hope: just alter the dreams* (2006).

In 2009 Cheryl was named New South Wales Woman of the Year, and in 2014 received the Medal of the Order of Australia for service to people with disabilities, their families and carers. Her involvement with disability services arose out of caring and advocacy for her son, Jono, who was severely injured in a vehicle accident. Cheryl continues to volunteer her time to improve health care services, which she combines with her passion for writing

Cheryl has developed a high profile as a speaker to a diversity of organisations and audiences from community groups to keynote speaker at the University of New South Wales Graduation Ceremony. Cheryl devotes much of her public speaking to advocating for the disability arena and the rights of carers.

Cheryl is married with two adult sons and is the devoted grandmother to two grandchildren.

In My Blood

A memoir

Cheryl Koenig OAM

Published by Wild Dingo Press
Melbourne, Australia
books@wilddingopress.com.au
www.wilddingopress.com.au

First published by Wild Dingo Press 2019

Designer: Catalin Furtuna
Editor: Catherine Lewis
Printed in Australia by Ovato

Koenig, Cheryl, 1960– author.
In My Blood / Cheryl Koenig.

A catalogue record for this
book is available from the
National Library of Australia

ISBN: 9781925893021 (paperback)
ISBN: 9780987381170 (ebook: pdf)
ISBN: 9781925893038 (ebook)

Dedicated to my little angels, Summer and Olivia.
May the poetry of genes that flow through
your blood fill you with the necessary courage
to do the things you think you can't.
To never give up.

Acknowledgements

Success in any arena is rarely attributable to any one person. More often than not, it is the coming together and the strength produced by teamwork. I was, and still am, fortunate to have the support of a wonderful team.

My love and gratitude, as always, to my sacred circle of family. Humblest and sincerest thanks to my friends, colleagues and expert clinicians, who each played a major role in enabling me to write this chapter of my life (literally or otherwise).

Warmest thanks also to Catherine Lewis and Iris Breuer from Wild Dingo Press for their insightful editing and continued support of my writing and my charities. Iris, who recently and very suddenly passed away, will always be remembered with special affection for the sensitive and thoughtful soul she was. I feel blessed for having known someone who lived such an accomplished life with quiet dignity and humility.

Special mention to Matthew Cooper who gave his time and expertise bringing my website into the twenty-first century; and to a dear friend, Christa Farrell, for her meticulous eye for detail as she proofread the manuscript.

As with *Paper Cranes*, making money out of personal tragedy goes against my ethical compass, so proceeds personally made from the sale of this publication will be donated to Sutherland Shire Carer Support Service.

Finally, and most importantly: Rob. Thank you for giving me your best when I was at my worst. And thanks for picking me up as I continue to stumble my way through this thing called 'life'. People live better when they are surrounded and connected to people who are important to them. You make me feel important. And knowing I am important to you is a powerful antidote to feeling sorry for myself.

As we often toast one another in our quiet moments of reflection: 'My darling, it's been a blast!'

Foreword

Early in 2011, I had the honour and privilege of meeting Cheryl Koenig and her son, Jonathan, at a function where both Cheryl and I were Australia Day Ambassadors. I knew immediately that she wasn't an 'ordinary' person and as I came to learn more about her and her story, I realised she was, in fact, an extraordinary person! We've kept in touch since that luncheon and when she asked me to write a few words for her new book I felt extremely flattered; although when she asked me to write about finding 'inner strength' I immediately thought that despite my degrees in psychology she, really, is the expert on this! Nevertheless, despite my protestations, Cheryl persisted and noted that my contribution would be valuable, so I humbly submit the following thoughts.

We all have inner strength. Some easily know what this is and find ways to use it; some (maybe those like Cheryl) are forced to discover theirs and use it to combat adversity; while others never know what wonders are hidden within their minds and hearts. I feel sad for this last group because their ignorance (and I mean this in the purest sense of the word) impedes their ability to be their best and to live their best life. Because how can we be happy and successful without knowing what it is we're best at; without finding ways to capitalise on what energises us; without knowledge of those inner attributes and positive qualities we all have?

I spend almost every minute of every day thinking about how to promote the principles of positive psychology, and at the heart of positive psychology is the belief that we all have core strengths and, that by becoming more aware of and better at using these strengths, we can live happier and more fulfilling lives. So, if you're reading this now and want to know where to find your inner strength … look in the mirror and look deep inside because what you'll find will be all you'll ever need.

Professor Timothy Sharp
Founder and Chief Happiness Officer of The Happiness Institute, lecturer at the University of Sydney and the University of New South Wales. Bestselling author of The Happiness Handbook *and* The Good Sleep Guide, *the latter being published in ten countries world-wide, and is a sought-after corporate consultant and speaker.*

Author's Note

'I can shake off everything as I write;
my sorrows disappear, my courage is reborn.'

— Anne Frank

When my 12-year-old son, Jonathan, was in hospital two decades ago, and I decided to keep a journal of all the microscopic improvements he was making, little did I realise that from the tattered pages of an exercise book, my emotionally charged bits of scribble would go on to become a published book that would offer hope and inspiration to thousands. And, despite repeated requests from friends in the literary world, as well as from medical colleagues, to write something in a similar vein about what I was then—some ten years later—experiencing, as 'it would help others going through comparable journeys', I politely but emphatically refused, blaming a lack of physical strength and expressive ability.

'What's the point', I would say. 'I don't want to write about this nightmare. Writing it down makes it all real. I don't want to remember this part of my life. All I want is to never again feel this way. No reminders of how ghastly it was!'

However, my main excuse, when pressed further, and one about which I was genuine was, 'There's nothing special about me, nor what I'm going through. Don't you know that one in three people are affected by cancer?'

I have now relented but not without feelings of trepidation, as I know from past experience I will need courage to undertake a writing project that will see me embark on another rollercoaster ride of devastating lows and exhilarating highs, giving life to thoughts and feelings that lurk in the recess of my mind, neatly compressed, compartmentalised, and possibly best forgotten. To share the language, the expressive thought needed to describe that ride, will give an authenticity to what has been. And, to be authentic I need to not only reveal my weaknesses but put quite simply, have the audacity to write at length about *myself.*

My first foray into memoir was *Paper Cranes: A Mother's Story of Hope, Courage and Determination.* It, however, firmly shone the spotlight brightly and rightly on Jonathan and his amazing strength of character, with us, his family, taking up the supporting roles. In writing this story, the spotlight unfortunately shines on me. I only hope I portray half the dignity and grace as that of my son. Most of all I hope that in writing my audacious truth of what challenges confronted me, perhaps *Paper Cranes* will once more flutter into your thoughts, your hearts—perchance fragmented, possibly temporarily, but effectively giving certainty to the importance of hope. In my humble opinion, 'hope' is the most important word in the English language. A word without which none of us can move forward. History has shown how great leaders have used it to inspire nations, and I have had the great fortune to meet inspiring people who trust in hope daily and use it to move forward in their own lives.

And so, a year after *Paper Cranes* was published, who would have foreseen what lay ahead only eight weeks after all the hype, buzz and media interviews that came from winning the prestigious award of 2009 NSW Woman of the Year—and brought about the elevated platform from which I could raise real community awareness of one of the most hidden disabilities of all—acquired brain injury (ABI)? Who would have foreseen that as I stood in the kitchen one morning opening my mail in the usual fashion, there was going to be nothing 'usual' about that day nor the previous week, or even the last two months?

As dozens of get-well cards fought for space along my polished teak dining-room cabinet, and sweet-smelling floral arrangements and vases filled to their brims adorned every table and sideboard, I let my exhausted and trembling fingers pause before tearing open the next card. I noticed the official emblem of the stationery of the Premier of New South Wales (NSW). I opened it hesitantly and slowly unfolded the crisp white paper bearing the same formal motif as the envelope. As I read and re-read the words of the Premier's touching letter, sheltered thoughts of mortality which up till now were neatly contained in the corners of my mind, surfaced unwittingly, giving rise to a self-pity that brought with it tears. Silent tears at first, but which quickly turned to irrepressible gut-wrenching sobs, wracking my already frail physique with a ferocity that surprised me.

Premier of New South Wales
Australia

Mrs Cheryl Koenig

Dear Mrs Koenig

I have just been told about your illness and am writing to wish you well. And really, what can I say? There are times when even politicians are at a loss for words.

It seems only yesterday that I was with you on that proud evening in Sydney, congratulating you on being named NSW Woman of the Year, hearing how you cared for your son through all those years in the aftermath of his cruel brain injury, how you wrote your book about your experiences, a book that has inspired other parents and carers, how you raised funds for other victims of brain damage and have continued your crusade for the relief of suffering.

It's a wonderful story. And what terrible irony, what mysterious working of fate or divine will, has singled you out for this latest misfortune? People used to tell us that suffering ennobles. And perhaps it does. It certainly tests our strength. And if anyone is capable of coming through this trial and emerging stronger it is Cheryl Koenig.

The subtitle of your book says it all: *A Mother's Story of Hope, Courage and Determination*. You have those qualities in abundance. The mother's story is now truly your own story. And with your countless admirers and friends, I am confident that hope, courage and determination will see you through. Keep fighting. We need our Woman of the Year. We need more like Cheryl Koenig.

Stacey joins me in wishing you the very best of recoveries.

Yours sincerely

Nathan Rees, MP
Premier

Prologue

'Are you ready, Chez?' Rob's gentle voice trailed up to our bedroom.

'No, not yet, honey,' I called back with contrived control. I stared down at my small suitcase which lay empty on the bed. I knew I should be packing but, somehow, I just couldn't begin. For to begin, might be to end. It was that simple. *Is this how my father and father-in-law felt when they packed to leave everything familiar to them—their homelands, cultures, families and friends, to flee a war-torn Europe and savage Communist regime, and travel halfway around the globe with just one suitcase? If this was the last suitcase I ever packed, what would I want it to contain?*

As my white tulle curtains billowed in the gentle breeze, I stared at the adjacent wall filled with happily framed faces. *They are all that I need, that I want … Rob, Jon, Chris … my boys.* I selected a frame that held the four of us on holiday in Hawaii, smiling naïvely as we clinked glasses; toasting the captivating sunset as it sent hues of amber spilling across the waves of Waikiki. An empty hook now exposed itself on the dove-blue paint of my bedroom wall. *That's how I feel: empty, exposed, holding onto thin air.* For a few moments I held the picture against my chest then I carefully placed it in the suitcase. I had begun.

As I continued quietly packing my thoughts drifted back to where everything had begun. Not when I was born. No. It had begun generations before that.

'Magical,' some said; 'Meant to be,' said others.

Whatever it was, the beginning of my future was certainly mystifying. As though an imperceptible hand had somehow intervened, guided, led me to here and now. A hand which had serendipitously woven a thread between three generations of two families and across two continents.

Then I remembered what needed to be inside my suitcase. The Letter. Reaching inside the white timber drawer next to my bed, I found the envelope. I opened it, slid out the paper and unfolded its fresh creases to read through it one last time.

Darling Rob,

When our eyes met and locked across that crowded room in 1975, in that instant tiny sparks illuminated the path to our coming together— to a conversation that would change the lives of both our families. You were 19 and I was only 15 when we met 34 years ago. Nevertheless, I remember it like yesterday. I remember how tall and handsome I thought you, with your smiling hazel eyes and burnished black hair that fell to your shoulders ... perfectly in keeping with the look of the '70s!

I remember the moment I fell in love with you. It wasn't gradual, but rather a feeling of being hit by lightning. I remember our first kiss and how it set my soul alight. There was so much about you to love: your wonderful sense of humour, your smile that told me all was right with the world, your knowledge of where you wanted life to take you and your unblemished perception of the world itself; plus, a confidence and pride that was tempered with an unassuming nature. And when your hand held mine, I had a feeling, a certainty, that all that I would ever need was in the palm of my hand.

Perhaps if I had known then, been given a crystal ball to show me what lay ahead, what heartbreak I would put the one person in the world that I have loved longer and more than any other through, perhaps I would have walked away. I doubt it though; the attraction was too strong. Since the moment in time when we stole a glance in each other's direction, since you first took my hands in yours and guided me in the dance of life—a star-crossed lover's dance perhaps, but as inevitable as night following day. Just as in love during our early years when the future stretched innocently before us, unmarked and full of promise, as when dark skies loomed to threaten and test us. And despite having had our fair share of troubled times—the most definitive being Jon's accident which shaped our world into two terrains … the 'before' and 'after'—things have one way or another always worked out.

But in case this happens to be the one-time things don't work out, I need to thank you for being the most perfect husband and the best father to our beautiful sons. I need to thank you for all the wonderful times we've had—how you've made my life complete, kept me smiling, made so many dreams come true. And most importantly, I need to tell you that I would never be who I am today, had our eyes not met, had you not held my hand.

All my love forever,
Cheryl

'Chez honey, we'll be late.'

'I'm coming.'

Yes, I thought as I zipped the suitcase closed, *sometimes it's from yesterdays that we find our tomorrows …*

•

Contents

1

Teardrops to the sea

Three days earlier: Friday 12 June 2009, 5:45 p.m.

'N*o way!*' I jumped up indignantly from the chair that sat beside the doctor's well-ordered desk to move in front of the square incandescent light that illuminated my ribs, lungs and other parts of my diaphragm. 'I'm *not* having that! Have another look, because there is *no way* I'm taking that!'

'I'm sorry, Cheryl,' Dr Peter said, 'but there is no other way to tell you. You have lung cancer.'

'What the … I don't understand, Peter,' I said as I stared at a large white blurry mass on the otherwise dark image of my lungs. I had taken to calling him by his first name as he has been my family's very capable general practitioner since we first moved to this leafy suburb of southern Sydney the week before Jonathan was born, 24 years ago.

Peter's hands came up over his face and he rubbed his eyes. As he slowly brought his hands down and stroked his strong jawline, he grimaced as if in pain. His gentle brown eyes appeared dewy, and in that moment, I actually felt sorry for him. He cleared his throat in an attempt to shuffle through the deck to find the right card to play, all the while trying to remain composed. 'Cheryl, sit down, *please*. I've faxed the CT[1]

---

1. Computerised tomography (CT) is radiography in which a 3-dimensional image of a body structure is constructed by computer from a series of plane cross-sectional images made along an axis. https://www.merriam-webster.com/dictionary/computed%20tomography

scan report and been on the phone to a respiratory specialist, who has confirmed the diagnosis—'

I leapt to my feet again, cutting him off: 'But it's impossible, Peter! I don't smoke, I rarely drink, I cook fresh vegetables with my meals every night of the *frigging* week … I *can't* have cancer! I am *not* accepting it!'

The rest of our conversation was a blur. I stopped caring about what cards he was dealing me, I just needed to get out of his rooms. I vaguely recall Peter telling me about an appointment with a respiratory specialist for a needle biopsy. However, I don't know whether I paid, signed, or even acknowledged the receptionist on my way past the front desk. I do recall, conversely, exiting the surgery in the crisp night air of winter and seeing my own breath before me in rapid little bursts of heated vapours. I recall getting into my car and feeling suddenly cold. I don't have any memory of driving the three or so kilometres home—I must have navigated the familiar route on autopilot.

Without thought, without tears, somehow, I arrived home. I calmly manoeuvred the family sedan into its precisely fitted space in the double garage of the Georgian-brick home where my heart was held captive by tender memories of innocence and privilege—life before the evening that changed the dynamics of my little family; the house whose common brick walls had become anything but common, but rather a castle, a haven, a place where special blessings, or miracles of a sort, had since transpired.

Seeing Robert's car already garaged jolted my mind back from the distant place where it had retreated, and confirmed what I had already known: that he was home with Jonathan, just as he was meant to be that day—a day that had begun like so many others…

'Don't forget I've got to help out at the 'Carers NSW' conference today, Jon. I'm dropping you at work this morning, Granddad is picking you up and then Dad will pick you up from Granddad's place on his way home—okay?'

'Okay, Mum,' came his compliant reply as he slowly dressed. There would be no rushing him, this much I knew, he was going as fast as he could. Always amenable and an ever-present blessing in my existence, my precious rose had blossomed into a charming young man—albeit with some slight imperfections—or 'mild physical and cognitive impairments' as the real world would recognise. But handsome he was, with his cobalt blue eyes and beaming smile that melted hearts. And despite a challenging life other than that he was born into, he possessed a wonderful sense of humour, keen intellect and charismatic personality that not only fulfilled my every aspiration, but most significantly, had managed to touch and positively affect, so many others.

As I drove to the conference I thought about the previous night, and how I had not slept a wink, as had been the state of play for the past few weeks, due to a feeling of drowning each time I lay flat; of literally not being able to get my breath and of a horrible rasping noise that was emanating from somewhere within. The previous night, when I had managed to doze off for a few minutes, aided by three pillows under my head and upper body, Rob had gently woken me to say, 'Cheryl, what's that noise? Can you hear it? I think it's coming from your chest. It sounds dreadful. Are you breathing okay?'

I checked my handbag to see if I had that scrap of folded paper Dr Peter had given me a week or so earlier: a request for a chest X-ray. Yes, it was there. I had been to see Peter, or one of his colleagues, a few times over the course of the previous months with various symptoms, the main one being the breathing issue at night. However, as soon as either one had placed their cold stethoscope on me and said, 'Can't hear a thing', I had practically galloped out, glad that my intuition that something untoward was happening had been misguided. I wasn't eating well, had lost several kilograms and I had a lower leg rash that, even after seeing a skin specialist three times and several expensive creams later, wouldn't clear up. My lower legs were also swollen with fluid, especially around the ankles.

But as fate would have it, the weekend prior to the carers' conference, Chris (my 22-year-old second son) was playing soccer when he was 'headed' in the face by an overly eager opponent. He came home with a badly swollen eye which I thought looked serious enough for me to suggest he go to hospital.

'Nah, Mum, don't overreact—it's nothing,' he laughed it off in his typically laid-back manner, as he brushed my hand away from tousled brown, sweaty hair that framed his tanned face. I had tried to hold his hair back so that I could take a good look into and around those perceptive hazel eyes, one of which was gradually closing, its surrounding socket red and swollen—eyes that knew too much about life, about loss.

Two days later when he began to lose feeling down one side of his face, Chris agreed to see Peter, who immediately booked him in for a facial X-ray. Afterwards, Chris rang to tell me that it showed he had fractured his eye socket.

'Bloody hell, Chris, that's serious.' I replied. 'You had better pick me up on your way back through to the doctor's so I can sit in on the discussion.'

The GP confirmed what was in the report and sent us straight to the emergency department of the local hospital, where the two of us spent the entire day waiting for expert opinion on the best course of action, finally, getting to see a maxillofacial surgeon who said it was borderline for surgical intervention. He advised that it would be best to wait it out and see if the numbness subsided over the next few weeks.

Sometimes fate works in mysterious ways. Had Chris not broken his eye socket and had I not gone with him that day to see Peter, I wouldn't have ended the appointment about myself, boldly insisting on having a chest X-ray. I was beginning to not only worry about the rasping noise, but I was so very tired from endless nights where sleep was becoming an elusive memory.

*   *   *

'I'm sorry, Mrs Koenig,' came a soft male voice through the thin cubicle door simultaneous to the sound of a light rap, 'but don't dress just yet—you're going to need a CT scan of your chest.'

'No, I can't, thanks. Not today, anyway. I'm on my way to speak at a conference and I'm already running late. I'll come back another day,' I replied chirpily.

'You don't understand, Mrs Koenig,' he went on. 'We've just spoken with your GP and told him we've seen something untoward on your chest X-ray, so he's ordered a CT scan be done immediately.'

'Oh,' I said, perplexed, wondering how I was going to get to the conference on time and not let Maeve down. Maeve was a colleague and Communications Manager for the 'NSW Agency for Clinical Innovation'—otherwise known as 'ACI' (an advisory body to NSW Health that works with clinicians, consumers and key stakeholders to design and promote better health care for the state).

'Okay, then, if you think it's important.'

'It is.'

Pulling the thin cotton robe around me and folding my arms tightly across my chest in an attempt at modesty, I followed him down the busy hall to the CT scanning room. I was taken inside immediately, the radiographer oblivious to the disgruntled expressions of several people already seated in the narrow hallway.

'Is the room freezing, or is it just me?' I asked to no one in particular, as the contrast agent travelled through my veins.

Without waiting for the results, I hurried out and drove as fast as legally possible to the conference function centre. My mobile began ringing almost as soon as I buckled up and drove off, but I refrained from answering—pulling over would waste more time. It rang twice more. Fifteen minutes later I was parking my car in the basement and my phone began ringing again. When I answered, a frenetic female voice told me that Peter had been trying several times to get me—he wanted to see me straight away.

'Sorry. Can't be done,' I apologised. 'I'm a guest speaker at a carers' conference and I'm already running late. I'll call by on my way home—but it won't be till around five.'

That was how the day began. It ended quite differently…

'Hi, guys,' I said feigning as calm a voice as I could muster. 'Had dinner? That's good.' I put my briefcase-style handbag down on the granite kitchen bench and turned to look at Rob and Jon at the dining table. They had stopped eating and were looking up at me bizarrely from their dinner plates.

Silence filled the air; my voice had abandoned me. I stared mesmerised and lost inside Jon's deep blue insightful eyes, then turned my attention to Rob's furrowed expression. 'What's up?' Rob said, concern in his voice, query in his eyes. Still no words would come. Rob stood and approached me tentatively, 'Chez, honey—what's wrong?'

'I…I…' *Don't cry. Don't upset Jon.* 'I just saw Peter.' *Gather yourself; don't be a baby!* 'He said…he said…' I fumbled with something inside my handbag, trying to stall for time. I couldn't say it. I couldn't find the words.

'What did he say? Come on, now you're scaring us! He's left several messages on the home phone earlier today. What's going on?'

Minutes seemed to pass as I stared through Jon's eyes and into his heart. We had always been truthful with each other and I knew I could be nothing less at this time. Then, like the distant whimper of a small child, I heard myself say, 'He said…I have…lung cancer.' There it was, out.

Jon's jaw dropped and he gasped out loud before slowly asking, 'Not like that lady on the TV ad?' In his tenor, the sound of fear.

'No, honey, don't panic. Not like that, I promise.' I looked from his shocked face to the other—my childhood sweetheart, my love, my life, my Rob. His perfectly handsome face and usual wide smile that still made my heart skip a beat when he entered the room, was compressed into a million creases by the weight of what I'd just revealed.

Without even realising, I had been crying. My face was wet, my chin was dripping. Rob leapt towards me and his strong embrace cradled me as all the cards of our carefully re-stacked deck in the 'new' game of life which we had so painstakingly rebuilt, came tumbling down.

'How can that be? *Jesus Christ!*' As he held me, I felt our tears meld together, and in a voice filled with anguish, his heart cried out my own thoughts, 'Not you. Not us. Not now. Just when we were beginning to see the light of day.'

Yes, we were just finding ourselves, our lost intimacy; filling in the empty spaces of our changed hearts with soft hues of tranquillity and joy as we settled in and adapted to our new roles in this disproportionate world. Roles and selves that had been altered by over a decade decorated by the stain of blood, sweat and countless tears as we worked tirelessly, sometimes eight to ten hours a day on Jon's rehabilitation, placing all else aside. Somehow, despite the enormous strain on our relationship, we had managed to put our two shattered hearts back together, leaving the broken bits on the floor. Over the ensuing years, we had formed an even deeper understanding, or closeness, that came from the shared experience of knowing what it felt like to be broken and hollow from the devastation of losing the essence of our bright, boisterous and 'normal' little boy. They say time heals, and it does, only never *completely.* You just get more adept at carrying on as the tendrils of time grow over the scars. Of course, the heartache never ends but it changes… It's a passage … and it's the price we all pay for love.

*   *   *

Did I have dinner that night? I don't think so. My next memory is of coming out of the shower, still in the same continued state of disbelief in which I had left Peter's surgery. A state of denial—a condition I recognised well as it bore semblance to how I had reacted 12 years prior when the emergency doctor had informed me that Jonathan's medical state was critical, and he wasn't sure if he would make it through the night. It's where you just want to bury you head under a pillow and slip under a thick blanket of defiance. You simply can't accept what you're hearing, because in your mind what your hearing is completely unacceptable.

Here I was with another dire prognosis, trying to keep my emotions in check. A pitiful and futile attempt to stay in control, because you see, that's who I was—Cheryl Koenig: wife, mum, carer, daughter, sister, friend, author, volunteer, guest speaker and *frigging* NSW Woman of the Year, whose ego had led me to think that my life was in control, that I was always in control, and that I controlled my circumstances. Never too upset, too sad, too angry, too satisfied. Knew to keep my chin up, not look back, only forward. See the glass half-full, smile even when I felt like crying. Hadn't I learned life's lessons the hard way? Isn't that what I'd written about in *Paper Cranes*? Didn't I infer that I understood the fragility of life and have the audacity to lecture others on how we should never let ourselves get too caught up in drama or we may fail to capture how magical life can be? *If that's who*

I thought I was, how the hell did I let the magic slip through my fingers once more? And how was I possibly going to control the outcome this time?

Walking towards the top of the staircase I heard Chris's key turn the metal lock of the front door to the house where Rob and I had spent the last 24 of our 29-year marriage. All but the last 12 years—since Jon was hit by a speeding car—had been as near to perfect as possible. Chris who was only ten years old that fateful evening, was now in his last year of a five-year degree in civil engineering. He had grown into a tall, striking young man whose self-sufficiency, independence, and innate common sense seemed to suit his quietly sociable personality. Chris lived and shared his life without flamboyance. A quiet achiever. An especially good son.

Whispering urgent voices trailed up towards me as Rob spoke to Chris at the bottom of the stairs. *Oh, no…don't tell him…don't hurt him.* I hurried backwards, away from the hushed tones of distress and back into the bathroom. Mindlessly, I began brushing my hair. In the mirror I saw Chris approach me from behind. He wrapped both arms around me and laid his head down on my shoulder. The arms that encircled me felt at once powerful yet shielding, as strong as the keen sportsman he had become; his embrace broad, protecting, emitting a need to keep all harm from his mother. However, his head upon my shoulder felt as delicate as the little boy he once was.

'You'll be right, Mum, don't worry. If anyone can beat this, you can. You're the strongest person I know,' he said in a voice that was anything but familiar.

'Thanks, darling boy.' I patted his head, then quickly turned away to hide my unwanted tears. 'Don't you worry about me, okay?' *Christ, why did he say that? Doesn't he know it's all a façade. I'm not really that strong. Now what will I do? How can I live up to his expectations?*

Rob rang his parents. More hushed tones of urgent anguish. Next, he rang his work—Alpha Flight Services—where he had worked for the past three years as a cabin service attendant, or catering despatcher, on international flights. A job at times frenetic and stressful due to the nature of airline schedules, but with his inherent work ethic, a vocation he had come to enjoy, and as such, had not had a day off sick since starting. He told Ramon, his boss, that he wouldn't be in the next day (Saturday), nor the next week, and in fact wasn't sure when he'd be back, if at all. Ramon told him to take as much time as he needed. *What irony, what craziness,* I thought, *would give cause for Rob to give up his work, his identity, for the second time in just over a decade? Hadn't he already proven his allegiance to family over work? Why, again?*

I went to bed, desperately wanting this day to be over. Perhaps if I went to sleep, I would wake to find it all a bad dream? Before long I got up again. I found the CT scan report, picked up the phone and dialled my elder sister, Amanda's, number. She was a radiographer. As casually as possible, I said, 'Hey, what do you think this person has?' and proceeded to read out the report:

The heart size is normal. The pericardium is thickened or there is a large pericardial fluid. There is a soft tissue mass surrounding the aortic arch, the left vertebral and left subclavian artery. There is a mass noted occupying the left upper zone anteriorly surrounding the bronchi and causing distal consolidation. This mass is continued past midline and continues into the sub-carinal region. Urgent respiratory consultation is recommended. And, the plain chest X-ray says the same, except they have the mass measurement at 7.5 centimetres.

'Oh, no! Don't tell me Steven's got lung cancer?' Steven, Rob's dad, was now 80 years old and, although once a smoker, had given up some ten years ago and fortunately, had never had a sick day in his entire life.

'No. It's not Steven. It's me.'

'That's not funny. Not even close!'

'I wish it was a joke.'

Suddenly my body began to tremble. I had had a low-grade fever on and off for weeks now. 'That's just what the doctor told me earlier and I just wanted to check it out with you.' My voice was coming in quickened breaths now, and I suddenly remembered all the recent times I had answered the telephone, only to hear the person on the other end ask me if I'd been running.

'I'm coming over,' Amanda said. I protested, saying it was too late; that she should go home to cook dinner for her 15-year-old daughter, Georgia; that I was going to go to bed. Before hanging up the phone, I said to her softly, 'Can you ring Dad for me and, you know, explain it all without the drama? I'll only cry and I don't want to upset him.'

I got back into bed and stared into the blackness. A few minutes passed and the silence was broken by the ringing of the phone. Knowing I wouldn't want to answer, Rob came into the bedroom and picked it up.

'Hello? Yes…yes. Okay, I'll put her on.' Passing me the cordless phone he whispered, 'It's Maeve'.

'Hi, Maeve,' I said, in my best controlled voice.

'Just rang to see how you got on at the doctor's on your way home?' she asked in her bright Irish brogue.

'Not so good,' my control suddenly waning. 'Apparently, I've got lung cancer.'

'Cheryl… No!' her voice changed from bright to stunned. We talked some more, then she told me she was going to ring Kate, who also worked for ACI, and was Maeve's senior colleague. Within minutes, Kate rang. There was obvious concern in her voice as she questioned me, and I answered with as much precision and clarity, due to my shortness of breath, as I could muster. Finally, she gave me her number on which to fax a copy of both the plain chest X-ray and CT scan reports. Several minutes later she rang back. This time her tone was more officious as she relayed a time and address that I was to see a Professor Brian McCaughan.

'He's the best cardiothoracic surgeon in New South Wales, if not the country,' she said, 'and his rooms are near the RPA (Royal Prince Alfred Hospital). He'll see you at eleven on Monday morning.'

All we had to do now was somehow get through the weekend.

That night, sleep was never going to happen—not for me, nor for poor Rob. He held me tightly all night; and my thoughts and silent sobs were for him and for my boys. *Why the hell was I doing this to them? How could I have let this happen?*

'Hey, Rob?' I whispered against the strangeness of the night. 'Do you remember our wedding song?'

'Of course, I do,' he whispered back. '*Moon River*. Why?'

'I can't get that silly old tune out of my head,' I replied. 'I remember Mum suggesting it for our wedding waltz and me arguing with her, saying it was too old-fashioned. But she talked me into it, saying it would be easy to waltz to, and she was right. It was easy to waltz to all those years ago, and it's been an easy waltz with you holding my hands, leading me, even when we've stumbled…' I began softly humming, then singing:

> Moon River, wider than a mile;
> I'm crossing you in style, some day.
> Oh, dreammaker, you heartbreaker;
> Wherever you're going, I'm going your way.
> Two drifters off to see the world…

'*Moon River* is like…our love…wider than a mile,' my off-key singing had turned to halted words and stifled sobs, 'We *were* like two drifters, weren't we Rob, 34 years ago when we knew we'd see the world together…and we have…and I'm so happy that we have—'

'Stop it, Chez,' he cut me off. 'Don't upset yourself, honey.'

'No—listen—I just need to tell you this. We've always been after the same rainbow's end, haven't we? Nothing fancy, just together, you and me, till we're old and grey. And—this is the last thing, I promise—thanks for being my best friend.'

'We've got lots more to do and see yet,' he said, softly '*and* I'm not grey yet! But I promise you, I will hold your hand through whatever happens.'

* * *

So many questions over the ensuing two days would come from family and friends. Stephanie and Steven, Rob's parents, came first thing the next day. I knew they would. They've always been there for us—the most supportive parents and grandparents one could wish for, especially since Jon's accident. They both hugged me tightly, pain obvious in both sets of speckled hazel eyes, as each brimmed with tears.

Dad rang from Melbourne, where he had recently moved to be closer to my youngest sister, Susan, and her three young children. I had encouraged him to move from the home he had shared with Mum for more than 50 years, as after she died in 2004, he had cycled in and out of depression.

'Cherie, baby—' he began, but couldn't go on. Hearing his voice stilted, wounded and cracking made me cry. I didn't want to hurt anyone, least of all my family. To think that Dad and Rob's parents had to go through this type of family torture, yet again, at what should be a peaceful time—the autumn of their lives—absolutely gutted me, as I knew I was the source of their pain.

Only a few months earlier I had sat down separately with my dad, Fred, and then my father-in-law, Steven, and asked them to recount the story of their lives. My purpose in so doing was my belief that just as our proud Indigenous Australians pass down their ancestral stories to keep history alive, so, too, must we—if we are to do justice to our label as a 'proud multicultural society'; to share the revelation of uncelebrated post-World War II immigrants whose lives were lived out with success, grace and moral purpose. Lives from which I have, and others could, significantly learn.

As well, my father and father-in-law's stories as they reconnected in Sydney was an amazing tale of serendipity. They actually knew each other as boys before the war, in their town of birth, Timişoara, in south-west Romania, close to the Hungarian border. They each considered themselves Hungarian, both having Hungarian mothers who, typically, loved to indulge their sons and nourish them with heart-warming Hungarian cooking. Goulash with nockedli (egg dumplings), capsicums stuffed with meat and rice, and other such traditional dishes were their usual fare at home. Both mothers instilled in their sons a strong sense of family.

Hungarian was the language they were raised with, and although from different religions and social backgrounds, their family paths crossed on a few occasions. However, as the war deepened and the boys grew into the troubled skins of their adolescence, their paths dramatically separated— with each waging their own battle for survival in different ways. They didn't reunite until 25 years later in Sydney, five months after Rob and I had met and thought it was about time to introduce our parents to one another. Naturally that day turned out to be an unexpected momentous occasion for both families. One of those unusual experiences in life where you feel something mystical has just occurred; a synchronicity beyond logic.

When I finally had time to mentally travel back almost a century to where this mysterious hand of fate had intervened, to piece together two families' separate yet combined stories, it was just before my unwelcome diagnosis. Each father was then aged almost eighty. Each narrated their individual stories of survival and escape, over several sessions. Their personal narrations revealed considerable dissimilarities and contrasts in both their experiences and recollections. My father's memory for obscure detail about people, names and dates was elephantine. Yet until pressed, he didn't want to recall or discuss what must have been a terrifying and highly traumatic time for a Jewish child growing up in an era of intense prejudice, hatred and then the 'final solution'. Whereas, Steven was able, as if telling a tale about someone else's life, to recount close to a step-by-step journey of his escape and was able to paint the dark portrait of his life in Russian slave labour camps as easily as an artist takes colours to a canvas. Yet comparatively, he was not as precise on names, dates and places.

Memory is as perceptual as it is subjective. We each hold our own truth on history. Our ability to file away particular scenes and retrieve them many years later varies from person to person for a multitude of reasons. Despite the sometimes faded and differing appearances of both my patriarchs' recollections, in the end they each proved to be as reliable as the washed-out colours that eventually come together to form a rainbow and forge a reality of what has once rained down.

At our third attempt at the interview and note-taking process, I was eager to get to the nuts and bolts of Dad's story: 'That's great, Dad,' I interrupted, as he wandered off topic yet again about minor superfluous details, 'but I really want to know more about your experiences growing up as a young Romanian Jewish boy in the era prior to the outbreak of the war'. There was a reason behind my eagerness—I had a premonition that time would not do us any favours. Little did I realise then that it was *my* time, not his, as I had thought, that would be in question.

'Yes, yes, I understand,' he replied, pensively rubbing his hand over the top of thinning silver curls as he was apt to do throughout our conversation, his precious little poodle, Coco, snuggled cosily around his neck like a collar. *It's hard to see where the dog's fur begins and Dad's hairline ends,* I silently mused.

As I searched his furrowed brow and awaited his response, part of me wondered if I was asking too much from him. I knew, though, that despite being in his eighth decade, and his arthritis played havoc with his mobility, he still possessed a razor-sharp mind and prodigious memory. Nonetheless, as I looked at his weary gestures, I silently questioned where the years had evaporated and where the young energetic father, who worked around the clock to put food on the table for his five children, had faded?

*   *   *

Saturday, the day after my ominous diagnosis, when visiting family and friends finally left, I went upstairs to my small office, switched on my computer and began to read through the prologue and initial chapters of my manuscript, *With Just One Suitcase*, the working title I had already framed in my mind. I read, re-read and edited—exactly what I needed to do to take my mind off my own woes. Writing had always been my place of escape; a friend with whom I could lose myself for hours whenever I chose to delve within its creative space of spontaneous thoughts and sculptured words. An outlet for my imagination, I suppose, like those who turn a blank canvas into colour, song or shape.

My love of reading was ignited by my mother from a young age. However, my love of writing came much later, in midlife, through my desire to share stories of inspiration. Through my need to let others know to never give up, that there is *always* hope—although sometimes we have to alter our dreams.

Sometimes it feels as if I write when I'm at my worst. Not only do I experience a sense of catharsis from a release of negative energy, but the process of writing is something I can control. And, more importantly, I have control over the end result. I deeply believe that reading and writing are essential to how our lives interconnect, in forming part of the conversations we have with ourselves and with others; where we can share our deepest connections, relationships, dreams, desires, losses, and sorrows.

Memoir, more than any other genre, is about handing over your life and saying: 'This is who I am. This is what I experienced. Maybe you can learn something from it.' It is where you share what you think, how you feel, and what you have gone through. And if you can do that well enough, perhaps somebody out there will get the wisdom and benefit of lived experience.

Furthermore, shared stories—as in *With Just One Suitcase*—bridge the gap between past and present. Shared stories are what link us to our common humanity by giving us empathy for others and what they have endured. Being the narrator of my family's sweeping saga, the more I wrote the more I realised I was, after all, just an outsider, carried along by the energy of the people and their stories of survival, whilst captive to a paradox: the allure of living a 'less than ordinary life' against a backdrop of fear and danger. Yes, I was an outsider, an intruder into a community bound by a dread that I struggle to truly understand because I have not lived it. The more I heard from Dad and Steven about the horrors of this almighty war, and its brutal aftermath, the more I realised that adversity certainly teaches resilience; that unfortunate challenges are life's greatest teachers. And, I understood more circumspectly, that families from both sides of war were profoundly affected as they were torn apart—men unwillingly recruited to fight, whilst others scrambled for life from the sanctuary of their communities, or even their homes. World War II radically altered the pattern of family existence, altered societies on a global scale, probably more than any other historical event. The separation, the fear and the loss were evident in the familial suffering across the globe.

Documenting family history is not just important, it is necessary, because insights from other eras take current generations beyond their experiences of life today. More significantly, I believe we have an obligation to *not* forget what went before. For every single life has meaning, yet each becomes invisible unless shared.

*   *   *

Once, being alone with my thoughts was something I craved, especially when my ideas merged and linked to form prose. Yet this particular Saturday my thoughts were disjointed, unformed fears that flitted around like leaves in the breeze— timorous, exhausting, resolving nothing.

My mind drifted to the title of the story and the implications for me who was about to travel to a foreign place—a hospital— alone and frightened, *with just one suitcase.* Certainly, the association of comparing my own journey to that of Frici and Istvan was extreme, however … *how would the contents of my suitcase compare?* Like theirs, mine will contain forgettable memories, but … I knew what I needed to do: draw from their example, find the same inner strength, the resilience to face what lay ahead. From them, I had already unpacked an invaluable lesson: hope is a good thing, maybe the best of things. *I must find hope.*

There was a fervour to my writing that day, that as yet in my previous works, I had never experienced. I now knew I faced a very real, yet unspecified, deadline. I kept transcribing my written notes well into the night until I heard Rob, and felt exhaustion, calling me to bed.

2

Through a glass darkly

Rob, my sister, Amanda, and I sat anxiously in the waiting room of Professor Brian McCaughan. How long did we wait? I have no idea. Were there any other people there? Again—no idea. The chair colour, the walls, the carpet … not an inkling of their hue. No thoughts. Barely any memory of that day, or the preceding day. In fact, the only lines of conversation I can actually recall of our meeting with the surgeon are of me saying: 'Can't you just cut it out? I mean the mass, or even the entire left lung? I can live on one lung.'

'I'm afraid it's inoperable,' he replied, with a seriousness that matched his expression. 'I'm not going to mince words— it's wrapped around your aorta and main bronchi of the lungs. There's fluid in the pericardium around your heart—you have congestive heart failure[1]. You need urgent surgery. But before I operate, which will be tomorrow, I need to do a PET[2] scan to

---

1. Congestive heart failure (CHF) describes the inability or failure of the heart to adequately meet the needs of organs and tissues for oxygen and nutrients. This leads to the symptoms that may include shortness of breath, weakness, and swelling. http://www.medicinenet.com/script/main/art.asp?articlekey=6972

2. Positron emission tomography (PET) is a medical imaging procedure that provides unique information about how an organ or system in the body is working. PET scans are mainly used to assess cancers, neurological (brain) diseases and cardiovascular disease. https://www.betterhealth.vic.gov.au/health/conditionsandtreatments/pet-scan

give me more information.' Oh yes, those words I remember verbatim.

And finally, probably the most important line from the good doctor: 'Your only hope is if it's a lymphoma'.

From Professor McCaughan's rooms the three of us immediately made our way towards the nuclear X-ray department of RPA, only a short 100-metre walk away, for an entire body PET scan, which would highlight any hotspots or cancerous activity anywhere within my body. As we made our way down the incline of the footpath, my legs felt weak and wobbly. I felt as if I was floating down the pavement on a thick spongy cloud. Fortunately, Rob had a firm grip of my hand to keep me in place, as through the pavement cracks I suddenly felt time disappearing. All the while, I kept whispering, 'It's got to be a lymphoma … It's got to be a lymphoma'. At one point I even asked Amanda, 'What the hell *is* a lymphoma?'

'Blood cancer. I think it's similar to leukaemia,' she replied. 'And that's right, just keep thinking positively.'

'Leukaemia? Shit!' Suddenly thinking positively didn't sound so positive any more.

Driving home from the hospital my mobile suddenly sung out its raspy ringtone: Rod Stewart's *True Blue*: '*Never been a millionaire, and I tell you baby I don't care…*' When I answered, Professor McCaughan's deep voice was on the other end—a voice that matched his tall debonair appearance, which in turn matched his courteous manner. He told me that the PET scan had told him exactly what he needed the next day: he would biopsy my lung, remove a cancerous lymph node in my neck and insert a drain into the sac around the heart.

At home that afternoon I took myself back to my writing room and turned on the computer. I stared at the screen. It stared back at me, waiting for a prompt. As much as I desired to explore my creative world of thought and opinion, I couldn't summon the necessary language or the motivation, to even read what I'd written the previous session. I couldn't quieten my mind to find the discernment I needed. All I could think of was what if…

Taking myself outside to find Rob where he was working in the garden, I asked, 'Have I let this happen because I've been too busy trying to keep all the balls in the air rather than advocate regarding my own crappy health?'

'Don't blame yourself, Chez—it won't get you anywhere.'

'Yeah, but would I have let things get this far if I'd noticed one of the boys coughing, or tired and pale?'

'Well, what can I say? You know the answer to that.'

Admittedly, for the past few years I had worked tirelessly as a volunteer consumer representative on at least six different committees in the health care arena, as well as guest-speaking at various medical conferences, corporate functions and disability support groups nationwide, obsessed with my newly found rationale to turn something tragic into something meaningful. I was fervent in my mission to change the medical profession's attitude, and society's (no less), towards people with acquired brain injury (ABI) and their lifelong ability to 'recover lost function'. It's now an accepted term and view which is widely recognised, documented and promoted as the brain's ability to adapt and change itself, or in common scientific terms: 'Neuroplasticity'.

Passionate in my belief that as a humane and caring society, it is only a lack of education, and hence a need to inform the broader community that most people with ABI are capable of returning to mainstream work or school. That people with ABI only need more tolerance and a better understanding by fair-minded business people and educators to be able to participate and validate themselves as worthwhile contributors to community life. Only through the integration of people less able are we able to promote a socially just community and thereby create community cohesion by including those at most risk of feeling excluded. This would significantly reduce the devastating impact of social isolation and the spiralling effect it has upon the entire structure of the family unit, often fracturing it beyond repair. Yet, had my relentless quest to raise this agenda fractured my own life beyond repair? Yes, I had been so busy with my new-found mission, as well as caring for Jon and trying to be the very best wife, mum, daughter, sister and friend that I knew how, that I, like so many carers past and present, put myself and my own well-being at the bottom of the pile.

* * *

'Don't you know who I am?' I joked with the anaesthetist, just before he placed the mask over my face to send me away to a place where fairies danced in the soft glow of moonlight. Some months prior, there had been a political scandal of sorts when a female federal politician had allegedly said to staff in a restaurant, when supposedly looking for a favour: 'Don't you know who I am?'

'Well, I'm New South Wales Woman of the Year. So, you'd better take…good…care…of…me…' My words began to slur, my lids felt heavy. The last thing I remember before drifting off were muffled peals of laughter from behind the masks of several blurry figures gathered around me, gowned in blue pyjamas and matching caps.

What seemed like only seconds later, I was awake and in severe pain. 'Nurse,' I tried to say as loudly as possible, but only a whisper would emerge. 'Nurse,' I tried again, 'I'm in terrible pain'. No response.

Not one to give up that easily, I managed to pull the device off the end of my thumb that monitors heartbeat. With an alarm shrilling, the nurse was forced to attend my bedside. 'Nurse, I need something for pain.'

'I'm sorry,' she said, 'but you've had your medication. You can't have any more.' And without even waiting for my response, she retreated from whence she had come, a distant blurred figure now in the far corner of the recovery room, incapable of hearing.

Some hours later I was transferred to a general ward and when I woke again, so too did the pain intensify. It was coming from the half-centimetre plastic drainage tube that was inserted in through my chest wall to drain the fluid from around my heart. Fortunately, the nurses were more considerate and forthcoming with pain relief here.

Other than looking up into some very worried expressions from my visiting family, I have absolutely no recollection of that night, the next day, or even the night after. My lapse in memory was similar to a condition I have come to learn about in my experience with brain injury: 'post traumatic amnesia' (PTA). But as I had not had the misfortune of suffering an acquired brain injury, I believe the more precise explanation could be 'post-traumatic stress disorder' (PTSD)—something I am not familiar with but am assuming that I subconsciously chose not to form memories of those distressing times. Inadvertently, I now had a vague understanding of the defence mechanism that explained my father's lapse in his painful childhood memories.

Two days later, however, a couple of important things happened that I definitely chose to remember. Firstly, the wretched drainage tube was removed. This was no mean feat as it was stuck and took three nurses—one with her foot wedged up on the end of the bed to gain more leverage—with each pulling and tugging, before the damn thing decided to let go.

'Ye-ow,' I said, not too softly. 'I'd rather give birth than go through that again!'

And secondly, and by far most significantly, Professor McCaughan came to see me with the results of the biopsy. 'You are one lucky lady,' he said, smiling for the first time since I had met him four days earlier. 'It's a lymphoma. Hodgkin's lymphoma to be exact.'

'Wonderful!' I beamed as I pushed myself upright. 'Does that mean it's treatable?'

'It's not only treatable, dear lady, but potentially curable.'

'Fan-bloody-tastic!' I suddenly felt a glimmer of light slip between the dappled shadows of doom—a light that had made itself known to me some years ago, in the early nightmarish weeks following Jonathan's accident. A sliver of hope.

As he walked out of the room, I reached for my phone. My first call was naturally to my darling, Rob. He was driving in to see me at the time of my call.

'What? Lymphoma? Chez, honey, that is such good news! Wait a sec, I have to pull over, honey.' Then, in a thick voice: 'I can't see where I'm going'.

Still on a high from the good news, I arrived home in good spirits from the private hospital that same evening. Being late, and in some pain, I took myself off to bed early. The surgeon had briefly elaborated on the next step of treatment to Rob and me prior to us leaving. Now knowing that we were dealing with Hodgkin's lymphoma—a general term for cancers of the lymphatic system found in the lymph nodes in organs like the spleen, liver, bone marrow, as well as other sites (and in my case it was the lymph nodes surrounding the heart and in my neck)—he informed us that he would be referring me on to his colleague from RPA, haematologist, Professor John Gibson.

'You'll be in good hands, Cheryl,' he assured me.

As the night progressed, so too, did my chest pain and shortness of breath. Not wanting to wake Rob, I left it until about 6 o'clock before I gently shook him and said, 'Rob? Can you wake up? I think I need you to call Professor McCaughan. The pain in my chest has kept me awake all night, and now it's become unbearable. It's right across my chest, from shoulder to shoulder, I can't move and I'm having trouble getting a deep breath.'

He jumped out of bed and stood looming anxiously over me. 'Do you want me to take you to hospital?'

'No,' I moaned, 'just ring Professor McCaughan. He gave me his mobile number—it's in my handbag.'

The surgeon didn't mince words, telling Rob to take me straight to the emergency department of RPA, where it would turn out I would spend the best part of the next two months.

3

My winter of discontent

Ward 7 West 1, Royal Prince Alfred Hospital, Camperdown, New South Wales, would be my address through most of June and July 2009. As the winter winds blew in across the plains of desolation (or rather, between the windowpanes and across the hard floors of this sterile ward dedicated to blood cancer patients), it lingered and penetrated, wreaking havoc on the lives of all those who shared this address. For me, each new gust slowly stripped away the very essence of who I once was, changing my view of the world and how the world now viewed me.

I was beginning to form a new aversion to the season I once adored, winter, which usually brought with it the majesty of snow-capped peaks on our country's Great Dividing Range. Skiing was a favourite pastime of our family's and had brought so much joy and exhilaration to Jon who had recaptured a pre-accident skill by re-learning this challenging sport despite his physical limitations. This was now the second time in just over a decade that I would spend the best part of winter in a hospital ward, and it was a stark reminder of how desolate and cold winter can be, even when indoors. I longed for the languorous hours of summer by the ocean and the mellifluous sound of playful, innocent, children. I longed for the restorative ambience of the sun.

From one day to the next I went from being relatively well—admittedly it may have been pretence at being well—to extremely sick, with the mass the size of an orange making it difficult for me to breathe, and too sick to begin any treatment with chemotherapy to rid myself of these malevolent alien cells, still multiplying inside.

Chemotherapy is the use of cytotoxic drugs—either intravenously, or less commonly in tablet form—to eradicate or slow the growth of cancer cells and is used to treat most cases of Hodgkin's lymphoma. The type of drugs you receive, and length of treatment, generally depend on your stage of lymphoma and your general health.

Lying awake within the cold, barren walls of my new residence in the dark hours of those first few nights after admission, literally gasping for each breath, I felt so alone and insignificant. And so diminished, so far from home and my boys and everything I knew to be true. On those long difficult nights when I was alone and frightened, the only lifebuoy I had at my disposal to keep me treading water in this foreign sea was my mind. So I turned to a form, *my* form, of meditation: prayer. Being raised Catholic, my prayers, whenever I dug them out and dusted them off in times of need, generally consisted of saying the Rosary, and for me the repetitive nature of this prayer evoked in me a relaxation that silenced my thoughts. An almost Buddhist-like meditative state. As well as the many 'Hail-Marys-full-of-grace' and 'deliver-us-from-evils', my prayers also consisted of a few hundred 'pleases' and 'thank-yous', with a little bargaining thrown in for good measure. Along with its companion, hope, when adversity strikes, sometimes all you have left is faith.

The other peculiar thing I did, as I struggled to breathe, was literally talk to or coach myself—just as a coach might speak to his players: *that's right Cheryl, breathe … nice and slow: in one, two, three, and out one, two, three. Make each breath travel as far into your lungs as you can. Feel your diaphragm filling with oxygen. And as you exhale, expel all those nasty little cells out of your body that are making you sick. Focus on getting through the next five minutes … There you've done that, now focus on breathing slowly and deeply for the next half hour.* And, so it went. Was I delirious? I think now that I may well have been.

I thought a lot about my mum, who had passed away over four years ago. I thought I could feel her energy around me, her hand gently stroking mine, just as she did when I was sick as a child. I talked to her in my thoughts: *please don't let anything happen to me, Mum… Jon needs me too much… I can't leave him. Tell God or anyone who'll listen that I absolutely refuse to leave him. I'm NOT going anywhere.*

Some nights alarm bells would beep on and off for hours, unrelentingly, like the sound of a child playfully stabbing either end of a piano; disturbing the isolating stillness and summoning nurses in blue dotted uniforms. Torchlight usually turned to full overbed lighting, rousing those who weren't already wakened in the room.

'Cheryl, your blood pressure is very low. Do you feel all right? We need to attach some fluids.'

'Cheryl, your heartbeat is barely discernible and only 40 beats per minute. We need to call a night duty doctor.'

'Cheryl, take these tablets. Cheryl, sip this cold water. Cheryl, we need to tilt your bed upside down.' Their voices were faint and vague some nights, and at times I thought I could hear my mother's voice whispering in my ear, soft as a gentle breeze: *'You'll be all right, ma Chérie … You can do this … I'm right beside you. Can you feel my hand in yours?'*

Images came and went at different times. Mostly dancing in the faded light of pre-dawn. For at those moments—whether through lack of sleep, social deprivation, or both—I felt most contemplative. I thought about what mattered most to me: happy times with the love of my life. We had rarely spent a night apart in 34 years of marriage—aside from the five months I stayed with Jon in hospital. But 1997 was the year we fell through the stars into an unknown world where days and nights had different meaning; time apart was trivial. Now, however, I had never been more lonely than lying in this bed without the warmth of his silhouette, his soothing voice, his reassuring presence.

Thoughts of Jon, my precious rose, were both blemished and blessed. But I had taught myself to focus on what truly mattered—which was the here and now—and to call myself his mother, made me immensely proud. No one said life would be easy, but no one ever said it could be this hard. Yet, as difficult as the last decade had been with so much at stake, I knew if I had to, I would do it all again in a heartbeat. And my baby, my Chris, I couldn't think of him without remorse for opportunities of a normal adolescence lost—whatever it is that 'normal' looks like—and the deep regret that his accomplishments took second place, appeared diminished in relevance because of Jon's needs. They were anything but small. Chris … my calm, sagacious son, whose smile could make everything feel all right even when it wasn't.

Would I think and live differently if I had countless tomorrows? I had never thought about my own mortality before. There was always time. Always time for everything when you're in your forties … or so I'd thought before the doctor's prognosis romped across my expectations, like a fire devouring my field of dreams. I understood I had a good chance of surviving this blood cancer—for the next five years at least—but my eyebrows were singed and now every step backwards made me think more carefully, deliberately, about the fragility of life.

However, with this contemplation came a powerful thirst for life. And as I struggled to breathe, and postponed my appointment with death, I dared to dream for my boys and what lay ahead. I was determined I was going to make the best of the rest of my days with them. I knew that fools count their fortune in gold and silver, and that five-minute conversations mattered more than five-year plans. I knew, too, that everything that mattered to me could already be held in my arms.

Alone with my thoughts, old memories came and went, too—family tales, my mother's proverbs, dusty images of a long-forgotten childhood…

'Do you know your mother is an angel?' an elderly man asks the six-year-old little girl with pale-blue eyes and loose plaits the colour of corn silk. As the stranger waits at the unsheltered bus stop located directly in front of a pretty Cape Cod-style house in the searing heat of a summer's day, her mother has sent her out to him with a cool glass of lemonade in case he's hot and thirsty. 'Take this drink out to the old man, ma Chérie,' she says. 'Don't skip, be careful not to spill it.'

The mother doesn't worry about the monetary cost of such gestures, that she can ill-afford to help strangers when she has five children to clothe and feed and not enough money for either. The stranger doesn't know he is one of many to be touched by that angel. And the little girl doesn't know that her mother isn't a real angel, as she skips back along the loose gravel drive lined with flame-red roses and breathes in the sweet scent of lilac wisteria vines that entwine the tall grey gums in the front garden of the house.

4

Keys of my blood

Ma Chérie—the French expression for 'my darling'. Mum said she named me Cheryl so she could call me that. And she did, often.

My autobiography, or identity, began in 1960. One of five children born into the Loew family, I was raised by an intelligent, feisty Australian-Catholic mother of Irish descent and a hot-blooded, sports-crazy Romanian father of Jewish heritage—a combination somewhat unusual for an Australian family in the 1960s. I often refer to my narrative as chicken soup with matzo balls and vegemite sandwiches.

I was blessed with two sets of very devoted grandparents, and although raised under the dome of Catholicism, much of my father's culture was imparted—such as impressionable family gatherings around my grandparents' table to celebrate significant Jewish occasions like Pesach (Passover), Yom Kippur, or Hanukkah. My Romanian grandfather's Hebrew prayers, him breaking bread and sharing wine in a silver goblet, are treasured memories. And, of course, I recall my Hungarian grandmother's feast of food which she usually let me help her prepare and which I now take great pleasure in replicating for my own family.

It was while I helped her prepare these feasts—mostly whilst I stayed with her during school holidays—that she sang to me her lullaby from days gone by. Entrusting me, if you like, with the keys to her past. And in doing so, keys to my own; for if we don't know where it is we come from, how will we know where to go? If we are not told about our ancestry, we are virtually robbed of our own autobiography.

Only now, though, after capturing her life story in my last book, do I understand the long-lasting effects of her troubled past, as a Holocaust survivor. Which in turn makes me a second-generation Holocaust survivor—something I never gave thought to during my youth. I think I was bewildered by her deep grief; a grief that never ever left her. After all, she lost everything: her parents, siblings, friends, home, country and her culture. The only thing she didn't lose was her ability to love—her children, her grandchildren; I knew I was very much loved. In writing her story I was able to put myself in her shoes, even just a little, as I understood this horrible master of stolen time—one which robbed me of my son's unconstrained future. 'The Catastrophe' that changed everything for us. In writing those early chapters of my book, *With Just One Suitcase*, I felt I was honouring her and other survivors' memories, and hopefully, sharing her burden of grief. Through my writing, especially as a second-generation survivor who unknowingly had the fears of my grandmother seep through me, just by sharing her brave story I literally felt divested, unburdened by assuming a responsibility to help others understand our ancestors' traumas. Hopefully, I also conveyed the realisation that the passing on of these legends to future generations is as paramount as it is infinite.

Stories were instilled at a very young age by my maternal grandfather, too. Pop was a tall, debonair man with an Errol Flynn moustache and a deep melodious voice—a doting grandfather who played endlessly with his only child's children. As a young girl, Pop fuelled my imagination with tales of evil giants wreaking havoc and the escapades of three young children (usually myself and elder siblings, Stephen and Amanda) who, remarkably, managed to save the day in his many and varied tales of good versus evil. We would often act out his fairytales whilst Nana cooked a roast dinner at our home on Friday nights—with Pop being the 'giant' and the three of us scallywags hanging off his legs as he dragged us through the house. Pop's charming trait of storytelling and his gift of beautifully embellishing a simple anecdote was a delicious part of my childhood that was passed on to myself and siblings.

Nana, I fondly remember as a kind, dependable and loving grandmother. Despite severely ulcerated legs, she would travel hours using public transport—two trains, a bus and a long walk—to get herself to our home each Friday. She would then spend the day cleaning, ironing and cooking dinner, giving Mum a day out in the city to get her hair done and shop. Whilst I was at primary school, I would run the entire one-kilometre trek home every Friday afternoon just because I knew Nana would be there. If I couldn't smell her cigarette smoke from the front porch, I would be bitterly disappointed as it meant she hadn't come for some reason. More often than not she would greet me in the kitchen with a kiss and a plate of vegemite crumpets, or if I was lucky, home-made scones with jam and cream. As I grew older, she would often let me strike the match to light her Benson and Hedges cigarette which hung from her bottom lip as if adhered with glue— going up and down, with a long ash teetering as she spoke.

My parents, Joan and Fred (or Frici, as he was called by his mother, and mine, too, when she was angry with him), loved each other madly. Theirs was a tempestuous love affair and our household was a vociferous and disorganised one. Mum was not the archetypical housewife of that era, preferring to immerse herself in books and gardens rather than cleaning house; and, unfortunately for myself and siblings, would not have won any prizes for cooking. From a very young age she instilled in me, too, a love of books. In fact, I would rather stay home from school and did, much too often, to read a good book. From the age of about nine or ten I was infatuated with Agatha Christie novels; using our 'little grey cells' to solve the whodunnit before Hercule Poirot did, was a passion Mum and I shared also.

Despite our house being two-storeys, seven people and a zoo of animals resided in clamorous conditions. Upstairs, contained only two bedrooms, one bathroom, and a small attic. Downstairs was an average-sized lounge room, separate dining room, a miniature kitchen with eat-in dinette table, and a laundry. My only brother, Stephen, was the eldest, born in 1957, followed two years later by Amanda. A year later I arrived, followed by a miscarriage somewhere before Melinda's birth in 1964, and finally Susan in 1966. Eventually Mum and Dad converted the separate dining room into a third bedroom for Stephen whilst the four girls slept crammed into the second bedroom. Naturally, in such claustrophobic environs, there were spits and spats (to say the least!) between siblings close in age, and over the years, allegiances were formed and broken many times.

School was not a place I liked, even though I was at the top of my class every year in both primary and secondary school and won many beloved books as prizes for dux of the year (and was offered a place at the Opportunity School, after a Year 4 IQ test, which Mum declined for financial reasons). I was really a shy, quiet child, and despite being good at most sports like my Dad, I didn't make friends easily. So, my preference was staying home, and I had a mother who was very lenient regarding school attendance, which I took full advantage of. However, it didn't affect my marks. In secondary school, where students were then assessed and graded in classes from A to E, I was placed in the A class for all my subjects, my favourite subject being German, followed closely by French. In the Fourth Form (or Year 10) School Certificate, I was ranked in the top ten percent in the state even though in the 'days absent column' on my report card was the number 66. I guess that meant I averaged about two days off school each week.

On one of my rare appearances at school, I recall my German language teacher being terribly impressed with an answer I was able to give which, apparently, no one else could. Why do I recall that incident? Well, in the first instance it was a miracle that I *ever* put my hand up to answer a question in *any* class, but mostly, because the teacher's words of encouragement left a lasting impression.

'Cheryl Loew,' her voice excited, as she scribbled my answer across the blackboard in capital letters, even adding an exclamation mark at the end, 'you are brilliant. We need to see and hear more from you. Come and see me at the end of term for a reward.'

From that day, I attended school more often (well at least on the days I had German). Having the assistance of a Hungarian grandmother fluent in German helped, although she didn't have the telephone connected and lived about one hour's drive away, so her help was spasmodic. 'Anyu', which means 'mother' in Hungarian, was the name we used to call our grandmother—a name we, and our cousins Rebecca and Annabelle, adopted from Dad and his elder brother, George. Despite using this term of affection for our grandmother, as children we were somewhat embarrassed by the phonetics of the Hungarian word for father—'Apu', pronounced 'Ah-poo'—preferring to call him Pa.

So it was my great fortune to have inherited adoring, indulgent grandparents, and not solely because both grandmothers were excellent cooks! For my Jewish grandparents' customs—combined with a twice-weekly dose of love and immense spoiling from my third-generation Nana and Pop—all subtly influenced my persona. How could they not? For at the cornerstone of both sets of grandparents' traditions came respect, dignity, kindness and an obligation to certain morals and behaviour which, at the very least, left me with a feeling of never wanting to disappoint them.

Only as an adult do I appreciate how blessed I was to be influenced by two cultures. As my Hungarian Jewish grandmother patiently and tenderly passed down her much-loved traditional recipes and traits, perhaps she knew that it would be my special way of keeping her with me, always. When I carefully dropped matzo balls into her bubbling sea of chicken soup (now known by my own family as 'Mum's Jewish penicillin'), stuffed capsicums with meat and rice, made her traditional beef goulash; or most memorably, helped create her (and now my) signature cake—a lusciously decadent rolled chocolate-cream *Doboš Torte*—Anyu was entrusting me with her legend. As we diced, sautéed, stewed or baked, she narrated to my eager ears her autobiography of treasured and blissful days prior to the horrors of war and all its inhumanity. Anyu loved to speak of her lavish home in Timișoara: their maids, their beautiful furniture, silver, linen and priceless china—all which had to be left behind when they came to Australia in the early 1950s, some six years after their two teenage sons fled the brutal communist regime.

Accordingly, Dad was born into a very wealthy family in 1931, and when the brutality, requisition of Jewish property and deportations to concentration camps were taking place under the Nazis, the family managed to survive because my grandfather was able to bribe corrupt Romanian officials (and thankfully there was an abundance of them during that era, or I would not be writing this!).

At the end of Year 10, aged only 15, I met my future. In the naiveté of my love-sick youthfulness, I was surprised that it came as a bombshell to everyone when I announced I was leaving school to get a job so as to start saving for our picture-perfect life together. I thought it would be blindingly obvious to all and sundry: I detested school and I adored Rob.

Both Mum and Anyu were devastated: I was their shining light academically, after all. Anyu, especially, was upset; she thought I would be a doctor, for sure! But an even greater surprise came when my German teacher rang Mum and told her it would be a crime to let me discontinue my study of languages.

Well, as the famous Lebanese poet and author, Khalil Gibran, wrote: 'When love beckons to you, follow him, though his ways are hard and steep. And when his wings enfold you, yield to him, though the sword hidden among his pinions may wound you…'

The rest, as they say, is history…

My mother's character and appearance were unique and beautiful. No short, fashionable perm for her. She wore her lustrous auburn hair long and wavy or piled high on her head if she was going somewhere special. Her taste in clothing was as colourful and flowing as her nature. She knew her own mind without caring what others thought of her. When she did make a rare appearance at my school, or on the even rarer occasion when I'd have a friend over, my friends would remark on how beautiful, how angelic she appeared as she floated through our house, avoiding the cramped clutter like a graceful prima donna dancing around a stage full of props.

Yes, my few friends were amazed, I think, because I looked nothing like her! She was tall, I was short. Her hair dark auburn, mine blonde. Her cat-shaped eyes, a luminous hazel; my blue eyes, round like saucers. A perfectly peach, delicate complexion covered her oval-shaped face, whilst my round face with chubby nose was olive-skinned and pimply. Beautiful, I was not (although by the time I was 15, my tall, dark and handsome young prince must have seen something of a butterfly emerging!).

Yes, Mum was stunning. There was a nobility to her comportment, not of birth perhaps but of nature. As I grew, I learnt that her actual beauty came from within. She was beautiful for the way she thought, her perceptive smile, and the gentleness that shone from her eyes as she nurtured her children (not to mention the many stray animals she adopted—a tradition she passed onto my youngest sisters, who would often arrive home from school bearing a stray dog or cat). So, our home was a menagerie of various creatures; at any given time: small dogs, large dogs, three or more (un-desexed pregnant) cats called our house, home. There were talking budgerigars, a duck, a rabbit, friendly kookaburras and possums, and possibly other species I've forgotten.

In the late 1960s, well ahead of her time, Mum's independent spirit was drawn by the undercurrent of feminism that burst into the public consciousness with the rise of groups campaigning for equal rights for women, and a passion to protect our much-loved local bush and river environment. For some years she quietly rode that wave within the confines of her small world. Indeed, I have a lasting memory of when I was about ten years old and whenever Helen Reddy's popular song, *I am Woman*, came on the radio, Mum would march through the house twirling a tea towel or duster in her hand as she sung the lyrics (which was the closest the furniture ever came to being dusted!).

The song became her anthem. However, just as the lyrics go, hers was a wisdom born of pain …

Yes, it wasn't until I began writing Dad's story, that I gave Mum's narrative much contemplation. As I delved into the early days of their capricious marriage, I came to understand just how much of a personal price she paid for any small gains made. Buried images, watercolour memories—some happy, others painful—came flooding back. Mum rarely cried, yet even as a child I could feel her suffering, just as I do now in the imagery of my mind. (Images are precious to writers, they are our magic. They are our connection from thought, to the written word. More importantly, though, are the acts of listening and empathising. Only then can you hear and become the voice of your character.) And even though it was Dad's story of survival I was immersed in, the voice of my mother definitely shone through; as did her indomitable spirit. Just like her personal anthem, she believed she was strong, she could do anything, *she was woman*. I would come to understand this mantra only too well, but not before sailing through the choppy waters of my childhood.

It's not something I like to dwell on—my childhood. I suppose we were a dysfunctional family, but at the time I didn't realise it; I thought we were functioning pretty well because I didn't know better. Now, however, I believe in many ways this dysfunction was actually the making of me; it taught me independence and resilience, giving me a core of inner strength that I could draw from throughout my adult life. Mum and Dad were certainly drawn into their own lives—so much so that we learnt to be self-sufficient from an early age.

Unwittingly a door has been opened to the past and standing before me now is someone I vaguely remember: a dreadfully shy and too-often distressed little girl who is terrified each time her parents argue fiercely inside the pretty house that everyone admires from the busy bus stop out the front.

A house whose volatile interior is at war with the peaceful exterior it portrays.

'Please don't fight, Mummy!' she begs, with tears streaming down her face. And, as her father threatens to: 'Walk out!'—a threat which more often than not becomes reality—the tears turn to sobs as she grabs his legs and tries to stop him leaving. 'Don't go, Daddy. Please, Daddy, don't go!'

She's too young to realise that he will be back, if not the next day then the day after, always bearing a bunch of flowers, always apologetic. She will smile then, the lonely little girl with the long blonde plaits, as she sees her parents kiss and make up. But each time he leaves, she thinks it will be forever—that she will lose the father she adores.

He works around the clock: double shifts as a full-time taxi driver and part-time two-up player, so she rarely sees him. From a young age she knows it's the gambling that makes her mother mad. Their arguments are always about money. 'It can't go on, Fred,' she yells. 'People are knocking on the door for money and I have to quieten the kids so they think no one is home! How do you expect me to buy food, pay bills, buy school uniforms, for goodness sake?' And each time her dad storms out, the sensitive middle-born child runs to her room and buries herself under her blankets to smother her sobs.

In so many ways, Mum was a woman ahead of her times. She was a 'greenie', or rather an environmentalist, long before it was fashionable. She adored the Georges River bushland surrounds of our home in Oatley and was concerned about its sustainable development. So, after lobbying to save Lime Kiln Bay mangroves, and showing an active interest in other community affairs, in 1974, she was persuaded to run as an independent candidate in the Hurstville Council elections.

She spent over 13 years as a councillor, including three terms as deputy mayor and one as mayor. She was patron to over 100 community groups, leaving many legacies in her dedication to and achievements in community work that is impossible to do justice to. However, one of her proudest moments, after many years lobbying successive state governments, was to see the introduction of 'blue lights' on guard compartments of suburban trains to improve safety for off-peak travellers, especially women.

During the late '70s, my parent's financial position improved with Dad acquiring his own taxi plates, which gave Mum the opportunity to finally give thought to what else she wanted to do with her life. It was entirely obvious to all that she was never satisfied with nor able to fulfil the role of 'domestic goddess'! So the seeds of her flirtation with feminism and community activism, combined with the opportunities that opened up for mature-age entrance to universities, enabled her to realise one of her dreams and enrol in a university course in 1981, majoring in Drama/ Theatre Studies. It was important to her to attain further education, and not solely for the qualification. Raised during the Depression era and suffering ill-health throughout her childhood—the legacy of scarlet fever—her education concluded at the age of 14 or the equivalent of Year 9 which left her feeling deficient in that area of life.

Sadly, Mum was forced to retire from active community work in 1986 when her rheumatoid arthritis and osteoarthritis became increasingly debilitating. So much so that from the age of 65 she was forced to spend the last ten years of her life confined to bed. Dad, then also retired, became her full-time carer—a role he took on without complaint and with great dedication. Aside from weekend assistance from various family members over the ten-year struggle, he rarely asked for help.

At Mum's funeral in 2004, a stranger approached and told me that when he read of her death in the paper he was compelled to come to her memorial service, relating an anecdote about a time when he phoned our home at six one wintry morning to inform his local councillor—Mum—that a large gum tree was about to be felled in front of his property. Within ten minutes, Mum appeared at the site, stepping out of a taxi (not Dad's) in her dressing gown, slippers, and a few loose curlers in her hair. She then virtually tied herself to the tree until the chainsaw-wielding arborist retreated in fear.

As an adult, I am, of course, very proud of Mum's achievements, but growing up I was a very reticent and easily intimidated adolescent (you wouldn't guess it now!). And if truth be told, I begrudged her her involvement in politics, feeling she was consumed with a passion to 'save the world' which took her away from me. Back then, I recall thinking: *when I grow up, I just want to get married and be a good mum, as well as a good cook and keep an orderly house, just like Anyu.*

And I think I did my utmost *not* to resemble Mum. But isn't it funny how, in the most intimate of ways, the experiences— the genetic code if you like—of one generation flows into the next? And unexpectedly, as the years of my youth lie in the distant past, after an often testing yet prevailingly happy life, here I am with beginnings formed from a medley of backgrounds—proud to be rich in culture, but even prouder to be more like my mother than any other person.

Now whenever I reflect on my beginnings, I make a conscious choice to draw from the 'well of happier times' experienced in that pretty house at the bus stop. To select from the album of memories, pictures of its rambling backyard filled with huge trees made for climbing, its enormous old mulberry tree where forts were built to guard against giants, and purple-staining berries were picked in abandon and abundance. Or the album pages containing magical Christmas mornings where sacks brimmed with brightly coloured toys and fancy-dress costumes ordered from Santa, awaited at the bed ends of each excited child. Children who, as they played with much delight, would never guess how much their parents sacrificed to make their wishes come true.

And when I look through the frames that hold my mother's profile, despite many years of undiagnosed depression where she became someone I barely recognised (especially during my teenage and early married years), I choose to see a strong outline of a woman filled with vibrant colours. I choose to see her intense 50-year love affair with Dad taking prominence. Theirs truly was a love story. For their love was not the *smile* … their love was the struggle *before* the smile.

And in the background of each page I turn in my album of memories, shaded in soft hues, is the constancy of a mother and father's love. Their life lesson to me was the wisdom to understand that parents can only do the best they know how.

5

Labour of love

Rob and Jon came to visit me in hospital every day. It was their visits, combined with Chris's, who came after uni or his part-time job each night, that kept my spirits from dissipating into nothingness, that kept me attached to my fond memories, to who I was.

'Mum,' Chris said excitedly on one of his visits, 'I've been researching Hodgkin's lymphoma—'

'Before you go any further, Chris, just tell me the good stuff. I don't want to know anything bad.'

'Sure, that's what I'm getting to. I think you'll be pleased to know that on average, statistics show there is usually around an 80 percent chance of surviving five years.'

'That's fabulous. Thanks for that, honey.' I didn't want to tell him that I had already been informed about statistical outcomes from other medical professionals, and I didn't know if he knew or not, but I'd been informed that as Hodgkin's lymphoma was usually a young person's disease— mostly found in 18 to 35-year-olds—my outcome as a 49-year-old was not quite so unambiguous, especially given the size of the mass that had collapsed my left lung, that left only 50 percent capacity.

My reply to the doctor who had quoted me the statistics was that I have never been big on *that* particular number game. When I had my spinal fusion 15 years previous, I was informed that I had an 85 percent chance of eliminating my nerve pain. Long story short, it didn't happen. And when Jonathan had been critically injured when hit by a car, we were informed that he had only a five percent chance of a good recovery. It didn't happen that way, either.

Of course, I was also enveloped with much affection and unsought attention from family and friends. My Dad had flown from Melbourne to Sydney for my lung biopsy operation and had been staying with Amanda. They came daily, bringing me special treats in an effort to entice me to eat, or luxury items to make my bed more comfortable. Rob's parents, Steven and Stephanie, also brought their daily dose of love, and being European, proper nourishment for me. And it was Stephanie who took home all my nighties to wash and iron with her meticulous care, as well as overseeing the domestic situation at home.

I was blessed as well to have so many well-meaning friends and colleagues who sent their messages and prayers, in particular, from my publishing 'family' at Exisle Publishing, who took care of all my author commitments and other speaking engagements at various conferences around Australia, which will never be forgotten.

When Professor Gibson had told me to cancel all my commitments for the next six months, I had thought he was joking: 'Surely, I'll be better in three months' time. Can't I just postpone everything till then?'

'Cheryl, I've never met anyone who sees the glass as half full as you do. Believe me—six months, at the very least.'

It troubled me deeply to have to let people down; it was unprofessional and so unlike the values by which I lived—

breaking promises, disregarding obligations. But with the kind assistance from both Exisle and Chris, who politely declined all my incoming email requests, I had no choice but to comply. What also concerned me was not having access to my computer to keep up the work on my manuscript. When I had asked Chris to copy the saved document onto Jon's laptop and bring it into hospital, he admonished me with: 'Mum, don't be ridiculous. You're too sick to be thinking about writing. Just concentrate on yourself for a change.'

In a way he was right, I wouldn't be doing the story justice, but the thing he didn't understand was that in writing I actually found, and lost, myself. It may appear as if I was concentrating on something or someone other than myself, but in essence, it was more about the distant place I could retreat to inside my thoughts, to play with words; to be absorbed in the abstract dalliances of the experience.

If you were to ask any carer what concerns them most, what keeps them awake at night, they'd all give you the same reply: 'What will happen to my loved one when I'm not around?' And yes, as long as I had been caring for my precious rose and his ever-changing needs, that *was* my greatest fear as well. However, watching Rob and Jon together, the way they cooperated with one another, the way they made jokes and laughed—sometimes at the most inane things that also sent me into fits of breathless laughter—the way, dare I say it, they both dressed in mismatching shirts and pants, all my fears were allayed.

I was given a unique gift as I lay desperately ill and confined to a hospital bed: the gift of seeing the future. I saw that theirs would be a union no human could divide. As long as my darling Rob was alive and well, no one else would care for Jon's needs.

There are some things that don't need to be said; things that are lessened in meaning if loosely turned into language; times when actions really do speak louder than words. And each day as I witnessed Rob's unreserved love and devotion, my load became that much less. In that most barren of settings, my precious rose blossomed—the invisible glass dome of love and protection that I myself had placed over him several years ago, was now anchored by paternal heartstrings. I knew then and there that if necessary, Rob would leave his job in an instant, without looking back, without second thoughts. Without even realising it, he gave me the ability to let go of my deepest responsibility, which in turn enabled me to rid myself of my guilt of being sick and, for the first time in years, focus upon my own needs. As weak and sick as I was, I knew I had to be strong for him, for them, for myself. I knew I had to dig deep; far enough to find that inner strength I had found to fight Jon's war; far enough to believe in myself and my ability to win my own battle. *After all,* I thought, *hadn't people from the appalling eras of war, such as Dad and Steven, all found the inner strength required to deal with far greater adversity?*

My surgeon came to visit me twice despite no longer being under his care, because he wanted to check on me and chat about the chapter he was reading in the copy of *Paper Cranes* that I'd signed and given him as a thank-you present.

'You remind me of my good friend, Chris O'Brien,' he'd told me on his first visit. 'There're lots of similarities in character, especially your positive attitude in dealing with challenges.'

'That's some compliment!' I'd responded, being familiar with the very compassionate Dr O'Brien from the television programme, *RPA*, and his own much-publicised battle with cancer. He was someone I had admired enormously from afar, especially after reading his book, *Never Say Die*. I remember crying when it was revealed he had passed away.

On Professor McCaughan's second visit, he said: 'I just had to come by again to tell you that I think *Paper Cranes* is one of the most amazing and inspiring books I've ever read. I was reading it in bed the other night, unable to put it down, tears streaming down my face. When my wife asked me what's wrong, I couldn't even reply because I was so choked up. I was reading the part where Jonathan spoke for the first time and you got him to ring his dad at work, and he said, *'Hi Dad…I… love…you…Dad.'* That was *so* moving, Cheryl!'

Yes, from the hundreds of letters, cards and emails I'd received from people who had read *Paper Cranes*, that's the section that usually moved people to tears, myself included. Especially when I think about how—if I'd listened to the medical professionals—Jon may never have spoken again. Mostly, I try not to think about what others told us. However, if I let myself sweep out the empty rooms of past emotions, there's no anger lurking in corners, just a few quiet tears to be wiped away. Tears for the life my son might have had. And lingering in the cobwebs is a continuing frustration, borne on the thought that perhaps susceptible people in similar situations will believe that because a person wears a white coat, they are all-knowing. Fortunately, with the new understandings of neuroplasticity, when it comes to brain injury, the goal posts are changing, so negative prognoses should be given prudently.

From a burgeoning folder of correspondence from strangers thanking me for offering them hope when they thought all was lost, three emails had a major impact on me. One was from a young woman who had fallen from a second-floor balcony and sustained a very severe traumatic brain injury. She was extremely depressed, feeling helpless and hopeless, teetering at a point where she wanted to end her life. That was, until she read *Paper Cranes*. Jon's journey played a catalyst in her change in motivation. No greater reward from writing have I ever received than her brief, yet powerful, words. To help another soul, another fellow traveller, is something to grab hold of with both hands.

And the other two emails were from clinicians who worked in similar major Sydney trauma hospitals which I have included here (de-identified):

Dear Cheryl,

I am a 27-year-old emergency and trauma nurse. I have just completed reading your wonderful book (in two days between shifts!), and felt compelled to write to you and thank you for the way your book has helped me within my work.

As an emergency nurse it is easy to lose perspective on why you are in your job and the significance of what we do—as we in the emergency department usually deal with two scenarios when it comes to brain injury: either the patient dies (and in all honesty I have to say I have felt relief for the patient and their family as the extent of the injury as per CT scan would mean the person would have been left in a persistent vegetative state), or the patient lives in what I believe will always be an extremely decreased quality of life. I have always struggled when resuscitating [people with] this form of injury due to this. And due to the nature of my line of work you very rarely see the rehabilitation side of the injury, hence struggle with the idea of somehow being partly responsible for the life ahead of the patient and their family.

I have been a part of the conversation you had in the emergency department, using the words 'contusions', 'bruising' and 'chances of survival' all in the one sentence. All the while thinking to myself this is cruel ... why can't we tell them the truth about these injuries, explain them properly. Why can't we give them the choice of continuing care or not as I have always believed the outcome could not have any true light at the end of the tunnel—maybe this is due to my lack of experience in rehabilitation nursing, or just my training telling me this is so.

Your book has truly made me stop and think about this reaction of mine, to relieve some of the guilt I have as far as my profession goes. When I first became an emergency nurse it was to 'save lives', and more recently I have been thinking to myself 'at what cost?'

Your book has taught me that I do not know the costs, and they are not decided there in the emergency department. There is hope ... and there is still a lot to learn about this type of injury.

Hopefully, next time I am in this particular situation I can draw from what you have taught me ... right out of the textbook of life and do the most important part of my job ... give hope in what looks like a hopeless situation ... be positive when the families of my patients feel there is nowhere left to draw positivity from.

As I was looking for your email address, I found that tonight was the night of your fundraising and book launch. Had I found out earlier I would have been there to support without a doubt and thanked you in person. Have a great evening doing what one of the many positive outcomes of your son's injury have been … for people with acquired brain injury having you to fight in their corner!

Thank you, kind regards to you and your family,

R.H.

Hi Cheryl.

I have just completed reading your book *Paper Cranes* today. It was selected by one of my friends for us to read as part of our local book club. I just felt compelled to write to you about the book. As a nurse who has worked at [major Sydney trauma hospital] in the neurosurgical ward, I knew I struggled seeing young people with horrific brain injuries. I did not last long in this area as I found myself continually upset and emotionally drained from what I saw.

When I started your book, I will honestly say I cried through every page in the first half. As someone who truly tries to empathise with people's situations, I would briefly place myself in your shoes and imagine this happening to my beautiful boy. I am sure you do not need someone else to tell you how sad and devastating even the thought of this happening to my son would be, let alone you and your family actually having to go through it and deal with it. I even seriously contemplated not continuing any further with the book as I was so upset. But then I sat and thought how you must have wished your circumstance at that time were just a book and you could close it, put it on the shelf and return to normal life. Then I sat and thought how you had no choice but to be strong and face it front-on as a mother does for her children and family. I felt I owed you, your family and Jono the respect to keep reading.

All I can say is I am so glad I did. I feel I have learnt some valuable lessons. Life is not always rosy, and challenges face us all in varied ways (some more extreme than others). Life does not always flow along a smooth path and as a control freak and always wanting the best for my family, I find it's a constant fear in the pit of my stomach that some misfortune may fall upon my treasured family members at any time.

I think what I learnt from your story is: that as long as I nourish, nurture and appreciate my beautiful family and friends—those who are dear to me and enrich my life—all will be ok. No matter what hurdles life puts up in front of me, as long as I focus on this, I will have the strength to love, find meaning in life and find happiness, no matter how life changes.

Whilst reading a difficult chapter early on in your book about how you missed the smell of Jono in those early days in hospital—I knew what you meant. I love the smell of my little boy, and as I said, I have smelt that smell of hospital patients … just not right! He was having his daytime nap whilst reading this, and through tears, I could not help but go to him, crawl into his bed and hold him and smell—his sweet little boy smell—what a mother does, hey?

THANK YOU for your inspirational story, for making me appreciate those simple things in life like holding my boy, and for giving me courage to deal with what may lie beyond, in life. I hope Jono is doing well and improving all the time. I hope Chris is happy and I hope you continue to receive much comfort, happiness and enrichment from what sounds like a beautiful family unit.

Yours sincerely,
N.C.

Yes, we were given little hope of a positive future for Jon (or Jono, as his friends call him). However, as I continued to emphasise at every opportunity given to speak on the topic of hope: of all the knowledge I have gained during our family's journey of hope, discovery and healing, one important fact remains: human development cannot be accurately determined by science, nor can potential be predicted or spirit measured. There is no such thing as 'no hope'. There is only hope.

6

Who are you, said the caterpillar

After some weeks in hospital, often spent listening to others who had walked this journey before me; others who had not only lost their hair, much of their bodyweight, and most of their dignity; others who were well aware that theirs was a battle that couldn't be won and who amazed me with their grace and acceptance of something that was so *unacceptable*, I was finally well enough to begin treatment.

Professor Gibson had already been visiting me, keeping me under his clever watch, making sure, with the assistance of steroids, that my lungs were getting stronger. On his very first consultation, he told me all about the impending tests, what they would mean, how they would help him determine the stage of my cancer, which in turn would determine my treatment. One such procedure would involve bone marrow extraction for testing to make sure the cancer had not spread there.

As I lay on my side, a local anaesthetic was injected into my hip. Next a small scalpel-like instrument was inserted through the layers of muscle over my hip and pushed, with some force, into the pelvic bone where the registrar then used a needle to extract some bone marrow. Needless to say, it wasn't at all pleasant, but Dr Sam, Professor Gibson's competent registrar, offered encouragement as he assisted his colleague and also, kindly held my hand.

On one of Professor Gibson's first visits, when we were just getting to know each other's personality, he must have thought me a bit too confident because he said: 'What you have, Cheryl, *is* life-threatening. I can't guarantee you a successful outcome.'

To which I replied: 'But Professor McCaughan said, "it's potentially curable"'.

'That's right. But let me stress the word, *potentially*.'

'Oh, *you* can if you like, but I can't hear you. I can only hear the word *curable*.'

He smiled wryly as he walked away. We got each other's measure that day.

And when the time was right, as he sat in his usual fashion on the end of my bed, he patted my lower leg and said: 'Right missy, tomorrow we begin chemotherapy'.

Professor Gibson was not a tall man in stature, but unequivocally immense in both medical knowledge and compassion which he brought with him at each daily visit, along with a very welcomed, comforting, bedside manner. From the outset, he wasn't afraid to keep arms' distance from what I'm sure he thought was a 'curious-looking' family. One minute he'd be talking sport with Rob, the next cracking jokes with Jon. Conversely, he'd be nothing short of professional when discussing treatment, and he wasn't afraid of using his stern voice with me when he had to—on just a couple of occasions!

On his advice, I was to undergo six months of six cycles (or 12 infusions) of chemotherapy, followed up with four weeks of daily radiation to 'mop up any leftover cancerous cells'.

By the time I was actually well enough to receive my first dose, I wasn't overly anxious or concerned with talk about side effects. I just wanted it to begin so that the healing could also begin. So, on a chilly Friday morning in early July, Simon, the expertly trained Nursing Unit Manager, clad in purple gown and full-face plastic visor (which came to represent 'here-cometh-your-lethal-cocktail-of-toxins garb'), took me on a nauseous ride from which there was no getting off, as he administered Professor Gibson's weapon of choice through an intravenous drip into his naively unsuspecting victim. Yes, I know, I'm dramatising it … but only a tad!

Actually, the first dose was the easy one. I was still an inpatient and was therefore looked after with every 'anti-drug' available, as required. Everyone reacts differently to their treatment; side effects are as individual as the patient. However, most people experience some or all of the following: nausea and vomiting, diarrhoea, fatigue, muscle pain, hair loss, dental problems, and more—the list goes on.

I was sent home the following Wednesday and, as Murphy's Law would dictate, that's when the trouble started. I'd left the vomiting and diarrhoea back in the hospital ward but in its place, I brought home a bad case of stomach cramp. I couldn't eat. I couldn't sleep. I couldn't sit. I couldn't stand. I couldn't walk without doubling over.

'I think I should ring Professor Gibson,' Rob said, concerned as always.

'No,' I replied, 'I don't want him to think I'm a big baby who can't handle a few stomach cramps.' And so I persisted with the unpleasant situation for several more days.

The pain diminished a couple of days prior to my follow-up visit to the haematology clinic for what was to become my regular fortnightly appointment for infusion of chemotherapy as an outpatient.

* * *

Every second Tuesday Rob, Jon and I would head out for a long day at the hospital that began with a 7.30 a.m. appointment at the haematology clinic for a full blood count. Jon would take a day off from his much-loved job as a picker/packer at J.B. Metropolitan Distributors to fulfil his self-described 'duty to his mum', sitting by my side, holding my hand, just as I had done for him in hospital years ago.

Every second Tuesday for the next four months the alarm would summon us from our cosy doonas at 5 a.m. to shower, dress, have a light breakfast then depart to fight it out for over an hour in the morning peak-hour traffic. About half an hour after my blood was taken, the three of us would squeeze into Professor Gibson's sparse consulting room, to be updated on the latest test results and be informed on what the day would bring (and, of course, we would discuss the outcome of the weekend's sport's results).

The following hours of the day usually brought about a prolonged period of waiting—my cocktail of toxins took several hours to concoct—in the sadly much-too-busy Sydney Cancer Centre's Gloucester House, where I was now an outpatient. So somewhere around mid-afternoon, every alternate Tuesday, I would be escorted to an unpretentious blue vinyl recliner chair in a long, cheerless room, lined with dozens of other unpretentious blue vinyl recliners, and hooked up to an intravenous drip, along with far too many random individuals whom the grave hands of fate had indiscriminately selected.

I always tried to present myself as a ready and willing captive, despite the knowledge of what lay ahead in terms of side effects, which included being sick in the car even before we made it home. And later on when my veins decided to collapse in protest, I tried my best to return the cheerfulness shown me by the exceptionally kind nurses and volunteer tea ladies. This was not always possible as one drug in particular burnt like hell as it travelled through my progressively roped veins, so unfortunately, my cheerfulness depended on what time of day it was.

My second dose of chemotherapy would be slightly tinkered with to avoid the nasty stomach cramps and also some neuropathy (or pins and needles) which had developed in my fingertips. As chemo goes about its job destroying cancerous cells, it also knocks out a person's white blood cells which you need to fight infection. So, each visit I was given a script for an injection to boost my white cells, which I was to give myself five days after the chemo. I was also armed with a swag full of anti-nausea medication.

Being very conscious of the fact that each person's cancer journey *is* different, and as such, each individual has the right to react in any way that gets them through their own experience with malignancy (as well as how they deal with the accompanying pervasive thoughts of mortality and with associated treatments), means that there is no right, wrong or same experience for any two people. Therefore, the side effects I experienced and my way of coping with them may not be the 'right' or 'best' way. Bearing this in mind I don't intend to go step by step through each cycle of chemotherapy, suffice to say *for me* it was as unpleasant as its reputation. Even if you are one of the fortunate ones for whom the anti-nausea drugs work—and I wasn't—it can cause the most debilitating fatigue imaginable.

When I wasn't tied to the bathroom eliminating toxins from my body, I was curled up in bed in the foetal position for most of the subsequent five to seven days after every treatment. During that time, I had so much trouble smelling or stomaching any food, I lost another six kilograms on top of the three I had lost before diagnosis, making my already slim build look emaciated. And when you're lolling about feeling utterly disgusting but telling yourself you're just a tad sick—and hardly, if ever, mentioning the 'c' word to yourself, family or close friends—seeing your reflection in the mirror resembling those depicted in holocaust movies, does nothing to inspire you to feel better.

Also, as anticipated, only ten days after my first chemo treatment, my shoulder length blonde hair began to fall out by the handful. I was surprised by the swiftness of the hair-loss process, but not perturbed by the actuality of what I knew I couldn't control. However, I do empathise with those who are, as no matter how forewarned you are, it can be a confronting experience when your brush or shower recess is covered in hair. I made a definite and intentional 'choice' not to let my hair falling out upset me, my rationale being that I had much more than hair loss to worry about.

Five or so days after the second dose of chemo, when I was feeling up to it, I called a hairdresser to the house, with an assortment of wigs in tow. I tried on many different styles, lengths and colours but, somehow, I kept coming back to the one wig that resembled my own, now departed, head of hair which I called 'Emily'. She was a sandy-streaked blonde with layered shoulder length hair. She felt familiar and comfortable and we went on to become good friends.

I instructed the hairdresser to cut the remaining patches of hair very short. Interestingly, nothing I had read in booklets about side effects mentioned that when your hair begins to fall out, it actually hurts. It literally feels as if someone is pulling it out by the roots. Even when it was cut very short, I had to smooth it all down in the same direction carefully with my hand before quickly placing my head on my pillow in bed as otherwise, if it was pointing upwards or slightly askew, it would hurt. And when it was all gone, except perhaps for one or two stragglers that refused to let go of an otherwise smooth head (which looked as ridiculous as it sounds) it was colder than I had thought possible.

In the starkness of the worst winter of my life, I would cover my infertile head in knitted beanies of various vivid descriptions that some treasured older friends had knitted me. And, as the rounds of chemo continued, progressively taking their toll on my weakened physique, I can truthfully say I didn't give a hoot how I looked.

Which leads me to the embarrassing question of whether I was a good patient? I tried to be, but alas I think I fell short of the mark, leaving much of the burden of responsibility for poor Rob to carry. And carry it he did so brilliantly: taking all of the phone calls, returning unanswered messages, keeping everyone up to date with my status, washing, cleaning, taking care of Jon's every need, driving him to and from his four part-time jobs each week, caring for me and giving me my injections … and most importantly, never complaining. Did I thank him? Yes, but not nearly enough. Sometimes, in the days immediately following a dose of chemo when I'd be at my physical worst, my patient and loving husband would tiptoe into our bedroom to see if I was hungry, thirsty, needing anything at all. Because I was trying my best to lie still in a futile attempt to alleviate the nausea, I would just hold my hand up and virtually order him to go away and leave me alone. This was not the person he knew and loved for over 30 years; I did not resemble her in any way, shape or form; she was alien even to me.

Then there were the times he would tiptoe into our bedroom to see if I was well enough to take a phone call. Taking one look at my exasperated expression, he'd know immediately how to respond to the caller. You see, I found it difficult to talk to people about how I was feeling. I was trying my utmost to remain positive and not talk about cancer, chemo or anything else related, because in the turmoil of my mind, with the chaos that had control of my life, I felt a need to hibernate until such time that I was *ready* to emerge with broken wings restored, with spirit intact.

One sleepless night, feeling like hell and in a desperate attempt to find myself again, I went outside into the crisp night air, looked up to the midnight sky dotted with distant diamonds and called out: 'Dear God, I thought you had shown me who I was, what my true purpose in life was. I'm 49 years old and don't know who I am anymore. I don't understand what's happening to me. Please help make me a better person, and please show me what it is I'm supposed to learn *this* time?'

Receiving no answer, I went inside and back upstairs to work in the soft glow of my computer screen; to the place that offered me both solitude and distraction. As I read my jottings and listened to my dictaphone speak in my father's gently accented voice about the chapter in his life where he met mum and their early years of marriage, I realised I needed to add more authenticity to the words and images that he had unwittingly revealed.

'Your Mum was so lively and I was so quick-tempered. Yes … we had our fair share of quarrels. But she was also very intelligent and had such a determined personality. You know, I can't recall ever winning a quarrel with her!' he laughs.

7

Wings that don't fly

August 2009

At every chance I felt up to it, I disappeared into my home office and tried to transcribe my notes and voice recordings. It wasn't easy, my mind often felt blank, my head often felt immersed in the thickest of fog. *What's going on? I thought. Writing used to come easily to me and now it feels as if I have a word-finding problem.* I would spend hours stuck on one paragraph, trying to find the right words, re-reading and editing, changing commas to colons, 'which' to 'that' or 'but' to 'however', a hundred times over before moving on. Then, when I'd come back the next day and examine the same paragraph, I'd realise it was well below par. My usual good memory, which I prided myself on for names, numbers and general knowledge, had also deserted me.

When the next chemo-Tuesday came around, thankfully, Jon, who now possessed the better memory of us both, asked Professor Gibson: 'What's wrong with my mum's brain? She has trouble thinking and remembering stuff?'

'Ah,' he replied, 'it sounds to me like your mum has chemo-brain'. Seeing our bewildered expressions, he added, 'It's an actual condition caused by the chemotherapy. Jono, you can look it up on the internet—there's been a lot written up about it.'

'The medical term for chemo-brain is "mild cognitive impairment",' Jon read out loud from his laptop, later that day. 'It can be defined as being unable to remember certain things like names, dates and events; trouble concentrating and finishing tasks; difficulty learning new skills; difficulty remembering common words or finding the right word to finish a sentence. Sounds just like you, Mum,' he said, concern in his voice.

'Yes, it describes my foggy head exactly,' I called back to him, wondering why I had to get every blasted side effect possible.

Another side effect I was not too keen on was being unable to sleep a wink the first night following chemotherapy. I had a sneaking suspicion that it was related to the late afternoon infusion of half a litre of a drug the colour of bright red poppies which was making me hyper. Unable to sleep on one such night, I silently slipped out of bed and tiptoed down the stairs. With nothing respectable to watch on television at that late hour, I dug out an old family film dated 1990 to 1994, and slipped it into the DVD player. It was an odd thing for me to do because ever since Jon's accident, I had been unable to look back at home recordings of a family living life in blissful unawareness of what lay ahead. It was too painful to watch Jon running around playfully with Chris: kicking a soccer ball in the backyard or rollerblading and skateboarding on the front drive; and especially, strumming his guitar or playing his piano with such fluid finger movements. All of which he could no longer do, or if he could, it was without the sophistication, dexterity and precision he once had.

Yet here I was watching them play, climb, skate and ski. At first, I found myself smiling as I watched the two of them so young, boisterous and carefree. Then without warning, I began to cry. But surprisingly, my tears were not for the son who 12 years ago had his destiny interrupted, but for the younger one: the bouncy, bubbly, cuddly little boy with hair the colour of sunshine, and big smiling eyes, who was enjoying every minute of being filmed.

'Look at me, Daddy!' he was saying. 'Watch me jump. Watch me dance!'

I can't remember him ever being such a camera-happy extravert, I thought. *Where has that animated little show-off gone? Did I lose his essence, too, on that dreadful night? Have I been too busy to notice?* Chris was now my introspective son who, like a deceptively simple song that reveals its meaning the more you hear it, now only reveals his true self to others with time. He liked things kept simple, life without fuss, just as he kept himself and his relationships.

Watching the faded film flicker before me in shades so subtle it almost resembled an old, black-and-white movie reel, I began slowly remembering each scene that filled the screen with remarkable clarity. These scenes of a laughing family from a happier time, triggered forgotten watercolour memories that had been delicately painted in the imagery of my mind. Memories, like yesterdays, fleeting in nature, to be treasured and savoured, because they can never be had again.

*   *   *

Two cycles, or four doses of chemotherapy completed, had now dictated a pattern of reaction after each. I was usually wiped out flat for the best part of the following first week, after which I'd re-emerge like a wounded butterfly from within the cocoon of my white bedroom, a little shaky, a little lighter, with susceptible antennae and not quite able to fly solo.

However, there were good days in the second week after treatment. Most days I managed to not only wash and hang clothes out to dry but take an afternoon stroll or sit outside in the warmth of the spring sun, reading and editing my manuscript. Writing Dad's story, especially his commitment to caring for Mum in the final years of her life, had made me realise that even though theirs was a feisty union, it was a union that stood the test of time. And although they may not have been able to provide their five children with the best of everything, they gave us the valuable lesson of appreciating and making the most of what we had.

On many occasions, during my better weeks, after a mid-afternoon rest I was able to cook a meal for my boys which seems a small feat, but which gave me immense pleasure. I have always loved cooking; the feeling of nurturing and nourishing my little family makes me feel complete. Cooking, like gardening, adds a certain tone to my thoughts, providing for me a sense of fostering. On the other hand, for all the nights I managed to cook a meal, there were twice as many I couldn't, and so I will always be grateful for the sustenance provided by my cherished mother-in-law, Stephanie, with her sumptuous meals and my other 'food angels'—in particular, my good friend, Sandra, who left a meal by our front door every chemo-Tuesday.

The day before my fifth appointment with the dreaded chemo, Professor Gibson had ordered a PET scan to monitor the progress, or my response to the treatment and to check if any other unwanted active cells may have decided to migrate to other parts of my body.

On the way to the hospital, I could tell that Rob and Jon were both as anxious as me. I sat in silent trepidation for the most part of the hour-long drive, vaguely listening to the radio. As we turned into the street where the RPA is located, I unexpectedly experienced that same eerie, yet comforting, sensation of my mum holding my hand. I turned to Rob and said: 'Don't worry, honey, everything will be fine'.

The next day we had to retrace our steps to the hospital and, as usual before the chemo, we were to see Professor Gibson. Despite a roomful of pale faces of people—some wearing hats to cover their hair loss—already seated in the waiting room, to my surprise, as soon as Professor Gibson noticed our arrival, he ushered us into his office.

'I've just had a look at your PET scan,' he began soberly, before changing his tone to reflect his wide smile, 'and it looks like it's a champagne night in the Koenig household tonight! French champagne, in fact!'

'What?' I asked, not believing what I was hearing.

'Your result is far better than what we had anticipated. Better than what we could have even hoped for at this early stage. The mass has shrunk considerably and there are no active cells in it, or anywhere else in your body. Look here,' he said pointing to the computer screen, 'it says you're in PET remission'.

'Really?' was all I could find to say in my stunned state.

'Does that mean my mum does *not* have cancer anymore?' asked Jon, excitedly.

'Yes. This scan tells us more than if we were to cut her open to take a look—she has no cancerous cells.' Then turning towards me, he added: 'With that extraordinary result, I've decided to cut you back from six cycles of chemo [or 12 doses], to four [eight doses], which means you are halfway through.'

An hour later, as I walked into Gloucester House for my chemo treatment, it was with a new spring in my step.

'Here she comes,' said one of the wonderful nurses. 'Our miracle lady!'

8

The best bad luck I've ever had

September 2009

As I sat in my backyard in the rejuvenating warmth of the sun on those typical afternoons of a lazy Sydney spring day, right by my side would be my loyal and beautiful golden retriever, Sandy. Now 13 years old, she was not travelling too well herself, with painful arthritis affecting her mobility. Like me, she had been slowly losing weight and becoming a frail shadow of her former self. Regardless, somehow sensing I was unwell, she would always follow me wherever I went, whether it was to the clothesline in the backyard, to sitting on our front porch, or wherever I placed my sun chair. And I was grateful for her presence as I sat and mindlessly stroked her soft fur, contemplating a season of new beginnings.

Kind people, some just acquaintances, had sent me books to help occupy my time. For the first time in my life, however, since my mother had ignited my imagination through prose and instilled in me a lifelong love of books, I had no inclination to escape to a fictitious world. I knew I couldn't flee the harsh reality of this 'yellow daffodil' society that neither I, nor anyone else, would ever ask to join.

My magical world of writing was still proving difficult, too. Prior to this health setback, even whilst caring for Jon, mothering Chris, cooking, gardening or attending to my committee and fundraising work, my life either consisted of writing, or thinking about writing. Such were the notes that played out the rhythm on the melody of my busy days.

One thousand, four hundred and forty … the number of minutes per day. We each get the same. Busy parents, exhausted carers, stressed business people. These minutes are, of course, our most precious resource; every one of them a part of life. The thing we cannot replace, recycle or reuse, is time. Does being busy justify being less conscious about how we consider the way we spend those minutes?

In considering my own life, taking time to examine what is essential to my completeness, or what is inwardly rewarding (aside, of course, from loving and caring for my family) I realised the value of having the chance to touch the lives of others through my writing and speaking occasions. So, taking pen to paper at every opportunity is essential. I have notebooks everywhere. *Paper Cranes* was based on notes I kept in an exercise book whilst Jon was in hospital—a journal about his improvements and our family's rollercoaster of emotions that I carried on for years. Turning my fervent jottings into a manuscript not only helped others, but unwittingly helped me realise what I should be grateful for and who I should praise, thank and do more for.

Actually, it wasn't until I wrote the final chapter of *Paper Cranes* that I discovered an unexpected yet very comforting feeling. It felt as warm as the sun on a brilliant blue day. I felt a new calm and an inner peace that I hadn't felt for several years. My frantic mind with its unrelenting quest for solutions found that the answer to my search actually lay within my own self. It was there all along, but I only discovered it through writing. I discovered a special place of understanding, and I was able to reconcile my pain and nostalgia with an unconditional acceptance of the person Jonathan had now become.

And like the turning of the tide, this enabled me to relinquish my attachment to the past. It enabled me to see that in many, many unexpected ways, we had been blessed and our lives enriched. From the depths of tragedy we were able to come out the other side with the realisation that we were not victims, but were indeed lucky.

* * *

As I pressed on with my relentless quest to form meaningful language, I refused to give in to the stranger with the foggy brain that now inhabited my body. I needed to occupy the empty hours that belonged to the vacant days that had become my unfilled, and unfulfilled existence. The actual time I spent at the computer, slowly turning words into phrases, into sentences and carefully into paragraphs, was, as it always has been for me, just a small part of the writing experience. What takes the most time and has always been the most rewarding, is the process of observation and reflection that lie behind the actual writing. And in performing this, at times, challenging function, I was exercising what few brain cells remained in my hazy head. And, as Jon had informed me from his research, this was incredibly important: 'otherwise, "chemo-brain" can be a permanent state'.

I wonder if Rob knows how frightened yet courageous his father was at only 16, I thought, as I sat and listened to a gruff and thickly accented, recorded voice speak to me about the terrifying time he was ordered to a Russian gulag:

I remember it like it was yesterday … climbing on an old open cattle train—my mother and sister, Hermina, with tears streaming down their faces, handing me a basket of food—waving goodbye. I was not to lay eyes on them again for nearly 20 years.

*　*　*

Emerging once again from my lonely cocoon, in one of my 'good' weeks, I took myself outside to enjoy some fresh air and let the sunshine penetrate into and through my thinly veiled bones, taking the manuscript to read over the last chapter I had written of Steven's story. In the account of his surviving three years inside a Russian slave labour camp, I wrote: *In order to survive and maintain his once-strong physique, he had to use his resourcefulness to prevent further shedding of weight.* How I admired the inner strength of Steven as a teenage boy and how I wished I possessed the same courage to think like him.

Sitting in my backyard sun chair amidst the budding spring roses, the glare of the sun illuminated the whiteness of the page, causing me to squint. The next minute shadows danced across the page as the sun's rays flirted in and out from behind moving clouds, making it difficult for me to see the text and therefore, equally difficult for my chemo-affected brain to concentrate. I gave up and sat silently pondering what it took to heal broken spirits. After what had been a particularly vicious week of illness, I was quietly heading towards another moment of self-pity.

As Sandy struggled to rise to her feet—her pain and weakness becoming more obvious with each passing week—I said, 'Poor Sandy-girl, why is this *crap* happening to us?' I knew I mustn't let myself descend into negative thoughts, however, after Chris had gently but firmly admonished me, just this morning. I had told him that I didn't think I could take any more chemo, not after the last week where I'd been so very sick. With moments of weakness so awful, I actually thought I would never make it back on my feet, and actually wondered: *is this what dying feels like?* Chris had taken me firmly by the shoulders and said, 'Mum, what's happening to you? You're losing your grip, your mental edge. You can't do this, Mum, because that's what you've got over most people.'

I knew I had to try harder: how could I disappoint my son who, like his dad, was trying to be everything to everyone? And, it was the little things he did that meant the most, like the countless times he sent me to lie down, bringing me a cup of lemon tea in a cup and saucer from my best china dinner set. The one we reserved for 'special' occasions. Chris made me feel special; made me thankful for his attentiveness.

So, bearing his wise words in mind, I took some deep breaths and calmly and quietly gave in to the serenity of my surroundings, surrendering all thought, all external pressure, filling my lungs as deeply as I could with the purity of the air around me. And, listening to the song of a far-away little bird, I had an amazing epiphany. I realised that I too could be like that brave 16-year-old boy in the gulag. There was nothing preventing me from finding the same inner strength and resourcefulness, like Chris believed I possessed, to keep fighting my own battle. It was just as much a psychological battle as it was physical, and the one thing I could control was my thinking. It came down to how I chose to respond to each challenge.

Like the last turn of a kaleidoscope where all the colours and shapes tumble into place, I was suddenly able to open my eyes to a new level of self-awareness: *I'm glad it is me! If one in three people have to get this wretched disease, then I'm glad it happened to me and not my boys. I can do this—and I will do it—in the hope that they will never have to.*

The truth, my truth, was that simple. I couldn't bear to watch one of them suffer through this. I realised that day, in the company of that little bird, that I was the lucky one. And I realised how hard it had been on Rob to watch me go through this. From that moment on, I promised myself to be a more appreciative and receptive patient. I would surrender to my new-found humility and turn away from self-pity. I knew that this self-centred persona didn't typify or do justice to my disposition, and I also knew that deep down my resentment stemmed from once seeing myself as the primary care-giver, to a lack of acceptance at now being the care-recipient; from not knowing how to receive assistance, but I promised myself I would learn how to receive and I would do it with grace.

That promise was tested not long after. I had gone to bed feeling okay but awoken in the middle of the night with a sharp unrelenting chest pain, which hurt more with each deep breath. *'Christ, what now'* I thought, but stubbornly and foolishly put up with the pain and the shortness of breath for several days, before ringing Professor Gibson. He told me to get myself into hospital immediately.

Amongst other tests, a VQ[1] scan was ordered, where it was explained I would have to inhale nuclear gas through a face-mask, after which my lungs would be scanned in order to detect the distribution pattern of the inhaled gas. Following that I would receive an injection of nuclear solution into a vein in my arm (if they could find one that hadn't yet collapsed!), after which my lungs would be scanned again—this time to detect the distribution of blood flow in the blood vessels of my lungs.

I was taken from the emergency department to the nuclear scan unit via wheelchair with oxygen attached, as I literally couldn't breathe, let alone walk very far. Waiting in the chilly area, Rob holding my hand as always, I was able to ignore the sharp chest pain as my mind was filled with other thoughts: *Yet another nuclear test! If I hadn't already had cancer, with all these blasted scans I certainly would have increased odds at getting the disease. Bloody oath, I hope it doesn't put me at a higher risk of a relapse?*

With the result of the scans confirmed, I was unceremoniously sent me to back to ward 7 West 1 with a life-threatening pulmonary embolism (a large clot on my lung).

---

1. A ventilation–perfusion (VQ) scan is a nuclear medicine scan that uses radioactive material (radiopharmaceutical) to examine airflow (ventilation) and blood flow (perfusion) in the lungs. The aim is to look for evidence of any blood clot in the lungs, called pulmonary embolism (PE). A VQ scan is carried out in two parts. In the first part, radioactive material is breathed in and pictures or images are taken to look at the airflow in the lungs. In the second part, a different radioactive material is injected into a vein in the arm, and more images taken to see the blood flow in the lungs. A blood clot in the lung can sometimes be fatal, particularly if left untreated. The most common early symptoms are shortness of breath and a sharp pain when you breathe in. www.insideradiology.com.au/vq-scan/

I was fittingly pissed-off at having to be re-admitted but did my best not to show it to Rob or the boys. *I can handle this, it's up to me to make the choice,* I reminded myself.

Fortunately, I responded well to the daily injections and steroids, and after the first few days I began nagging Professor Gibson to let me go home. 'I'm not stupid,' I told him, 'I know how to look after myself'.

'Cheryl, what do I have to do to get through your thick skull that you have a life-threatening condition on top of a life-threatening disease?' he replied, sternly.

Lying there in my hospital bed I found the days long and tedious. I was unable to read, do crosswords, or focus on anything other than flip mindlessly through magazines or occasionally watch images flicker across the small TV monitor. I couldn't help but feel institutionalised. No matter how hard I tried to think positively, I still felt like I was losing my identity, nothing more than a number over a bed. *If you think you've got it bad, wake up to yourself,* I admonished myself as I thought about the millions of people who truly *had* lost their identity during World War II; those who had become literal numbers—who today only had to look at the permanent ink engraved into their skin as a harsh reminder of how inconsequential their lives were once considered.

Nevertheless, by the second week I desperately longed to go home to be nourished and sustained by my family, to feel needed, to cook for them.

The phone beside my bed interrupted my thoughts. 'Is that Cheryl Koenig, famous author and woman of the year?'

'Shut up, Glenn,' I replied.

'Good. You're still alive. Thought so, as I hadn't read your name in the obituaries—but just checking to make sure!'

'Yeah, I'm still kicking. But when am I going to get to see you again, I mean in person, not just on TV? You're always so busy that by the time I see you, my bald head will have shoulder length hair again!'

Glenn Wheeler, media personality and all-round top Aussie bloke (who features in the final chapters of *Paper Cranes* when Jon was experiencing some workplace discrimination and he came to our rescue), had become a treasured friend to our family; his frequent calls would always lift my spirits. On this particular day, his timing was spot-on and as usual, just the right medicine.

'And by the way,' I added, 'I'm lying here on my deathbed and every time I turn on the blasted TV, there you are doing infomercials for those bloody funeral plan insurance companies!'

9

The gift of today

October 2009

Despite occasional thoughts to the contrary, just like so many other chance individuals before and after me, I made it through the ghastly rigours of chemotherapy. I was given a two-week break, after which I would begin four weeks of daily radiation to the neck and chest area.

As it happened, our thirtieth wedding anniversary fell within this lay period, and my indulgent husband surprised me with a three-day getaway to Port Douglas, on the tropical north coast of Queensland. We had a wonderful time; only a few days, but days that transported us into a sensory stimulating atmosphere of nature at its most therapeutic. The heat of the sultry days, cooled by the coastal breeze and tropical showers, plus the breathtaking scenery under the tall canopy of the Daintree Rainforest with its stunning walking tracks, cascading waterfalls and refreshing swimming holes— all combined to create a healing ambience that did me the world of good.

I had lots of reasons to celebrate, lots of hats to cover my still bald head, but most of all, lots of love and happy times to share amongst the three of us. Yes, of course Jon came too— would anyone expect anything else? Oh, and I mustn't forget the lovely little trinket I received: a half-carat diamond ring, which formed the zenith on the perfectly iced cake.

As was becoming a customary rhythm to our lives, the serenity was broken when we arrived home to find Sandy-girl had deteriorated and was now having mini-strokes, up to four or five times a day. Over the course of the following two weeks, the strokes became longer in duration and she was walking skew-whiff and sometimes losing balance and falling to the ground. We knew we couldn't watch her suffer, but it was just so hard to make the final call. Rob rang the vet several times, asking her advice, and each time she would give the same answer, 'I can't tell you when it's time. Only you can make that decision.'

We made the decision, just as adults are supposed to, before I commenced the daily hour-long trips to and from radiotherapy at the RPA. Sandy's final day was spent with us, her family, gathered around her in the backyard feeding her treats of cold slices of meat and sweet biscuits. I dug out one of Jon's old doona covers that had his smell washed into its faded colours and spread it over the grass for us all to lie down with her. To all appearances we may have been fussing over 'just a dog' but she was a *very* special dog, with the ability to understand a wide range of vocabulary. I could send her 'to the back door' or 'to the side door' or 'to find Daddy', 'go to Jon', 'go to Chris', plus so much more; and she had been a prized member of our family for over 13 years.

The vet arrived in the afternoon with her bag and stretcher, and soon after administered the lethal injection. Sandy took a deep breath and then gently laid her head down in Rob's hands as she exhaled her final sigh. The inevitability and finality of death stared us all in the face that day. As the sun bid farewell to the most brilliant of spring days, so too did we bid farewell to our most brilliant dog. As Jon and Rob helped carry her out to the vet's car on the stretcher, I ran upstairs to my bedroom and cried for hours. But it was Rob who cried on and off for days, whenever memories of her were evoked, as he was the one who patiently cared for her in her geriatric state whilst at the same time caring for me in a not too dissimilar state.

It took Jon's words of wisdom to help us move on. One evening as Rob and I both shed a quiet tear as we scraped our food-scraps into the garbage bin—where previously we simply had to rattle cutlery upon plate to bring Sandy front and centre—Jon said 'Mum and Dad, life is like a book. You have to keep turning the pages to get to the next chapter.'

So much happened in that two-week break between therapies, celebrating one week, crying the next. However, there was still one outstanding item on my 'to-do' list that I wanted to tick off. A talk as a guest speaker at an important function that I had been scheduled to make in August but had cancelled when diagnosed with blood cancer. 'The law firm, Slater and Gordon, had selected me to speak in my capacity as '2009 NSW Woman of the Year', as part of their inaugural 'Inspiring Women Series'. It was indeed an honour to be asked, so I didn't want the year to pass without fulfilling this special commitment whilst the award, or title, was still relevant. However, the main reason I chose to commit to this talk during my break between therapies, was because even though I had never met the chairman of the board, Anna Booth, she had phoned constantly since finding out about my illness. She was genuine in her concern for not only me, but Rob and the family.

So, donning my lacquered 'Emily' tresses—which I had worn only twice in the preceding four months—Jon, Rob, his parents Steven and Stephanie, my sister Amanda, my food-angels Sandra and her husband Richard, all accompanied me into Cockle Bay Wharf for a day I will always remember. The picture-perfect view from the function centre overlooking Darling Harbour with its billiard-table smooth sapphire waters, cast a tranquil atmosphere over the many gathered on the wide veranda, where we sipped champagne and enjoyed elegant canapés before moving inside for the start of the function. It was attended by a cross-section of leaders in their field: lawyers, politicians, financiers, along with Tanya Plibersek, Federal Minister for the Status of Women [who would go on to become the Deputy Leader of the Opposition and, being the daughter of immigrants, had also graciously written an endorsement for the back cover of *With Just One Suitcase*].

And I have to mention one other dignitary who would go on to become a significant person in our lives, who introduced herself at the end of my speech: Sarah Schoonwater, Secretary of the ACT branch of the CFMEU (Construction, Forestry, Mining, Energy Union).

That day, my first public appearance, I spoke from the heart with a truth and an earnestness about the important role I believe women play within society—from boardrooms to government to shaping the home environment. I also used the opportunity to publicly thank Rob and my 'support team' for their unreserved love and patience with me—and in so doing must have touched all those present (or perhaps 'Emily' and my make-up did little to conceal my feeble appearance), because as my speech ended, like a wave rising from the back of the ocean to form a crest, so too did a sea of strangers stand in rousing applause from the back of the room forward—table by table, all 200 people.

I looked at Rob who stood proud as punch, clapping loudest of all, with tears running down his face. (That wasn't my first, nor last standing ovation, but it was certainly one of the most moving to me.)

Seated at my table once more, signing copies of *Paper Cranes,* and having photos taken with guests, it seemed as if the line of people that snaked around the tables had no end. I was beginning to wane but refused to give in, not wanting to disappoint people who had waited to speak with me. Apparently, the Secretary of the CFMEU had waited as long as she could, before deciding to speak with Rob and Jon to let them know she had to leave for a flight back to Canberra. They quickly discussed rugby league football teams and, as she had once lived in the Shire we currently resided in, she asked Jon if he barracked for the Cronulla Sharks. Always the diplomat, he replied in the affirmative (which I may as well state up front is not quite correct—he is first and foremost a Canterbury Bulldogs supporter), and she went on to say that when the Sharks next played the Canberra Raiders (for whom the CFMEU were a major sponsor), she would organise a special trip down to Canberra for our family to watch the game from their corporate box.

True to her word, Sarah emailed me within a week. Jon, as he so very often does, had made an impact on her. Over the course of the week, she had given it some thought and came up with the suggestion that we should organise a charity match to raise some much-needed community awareness about brain injury and the impact of stories like Jon's, on families, friends and communities. And so, the wheels were slowly set in motion for a game that would take place in the middle of 2010.

10

Not over till the final whistle blows

November 2009

Radiotherapy began with feelings of trepidation. The expert warnings from the medical staff trained in this field were necessary, yet daunting: 'Your skin will get burnt, red and sore like bad sunburn. After about two weeks you may not be able to swallow food, as we'll be irradiating your neck and diaphragm and it could burn through and inflame your oesophagus. You may need strong pain relief to eat and sleep. You may get very tired.' These warnings need to be said, people need to be informed, but just as the chemotherapy affects people in different ways, so too must radiotherapy have its variables, and for once I was very fortunate *not* to experience side effects. I did have some mild swallowing difficulty, but it was right at the very end of treatment and lasted only a couple of days.

On the first visit to the radiation centre I was measured and tattooed with three permanent dots that would be used by radiation technicians to align me with the laser-like red beam on each daily session, over the course of the next four weeks. *Now I, too, will have my enduring reminder of this period of my life just like prisoners of war*, I was thinking as the black ink stained my skin.

Radiotherapy is the use of high-energy gamma rays or electrons to destroy cancer cells. It is usually given as numerous small doses over several days or weeks, depending on the type of cancer you have and its size and stage. The machine itself resembles a CT scanner or large X-ray machine, and you are either strapped in place, or told not to move, as the precision of the gamma rays is paramount. Similar to chemotherapy, the more intensive (or toxic) the treatment, the greater the likelihood for survival but the implication of the toxicity also increases, compromising long-term quality of life (as I would later discover).

However, it was whilst I was strapped under this large dispatcher of gamma rays in a horizontal position—every day for twenty days—and the intimidating red laser beam went about painlessly penetrating my being on its silent but fervent path of destruction, I again used the only tool I possessed to not allow myself to be frightened: my mind. I suppose it was a crude form of visualisation, but as the machine made its way progressively around my neck, chest and back, I told myself that I wouldn't get burnt, there was nothing to burn me, as in my mind's eye I was lying on my favourite beach—Broadbeach in Queensland—at the water's edge, letting the cool aqua surf splash over my neck and chest and trickle down my back as I rolled over in my illusory state.

It was something that came back to me from childhood. Something Mum used to say whenever I had managed to scorch myself whilst ironing Dad's shirts or my uniform for my first job as a pharmacy assistant. Or at other times such as carelessly taking something hot out of the oven: *'Don't think about the burn, Cherie. Run your hand under cold water and imagine it hasn't even happened.'*

'Despite Mum's early rudimentary form of visualisation, research[1] today has suggested that treatment including hypnotherapy and visualisation as beneficial in the management of burns patients. Have I mentioned Mum was a woman ahead of her times?'

I also did another peculiar thing: I visualised my mother's elegant, long-fingered hands taking hold of the black mangled mass in my lungs, and decisively crushing it, sending every last cancerous cell slowly and surely into smithereens. No sooner had I dreamt this dream into play, then the technicians would re-enter and tell me the procedure was over.

'You were quick,' Rob would say, echoing my own thoughts. 'All done?'

'Yep, medium rare on both sides,' was the most humour I could muster.

Rob took me to all but three days of the 20 sessions, as his employer had rung and asked him to come back into work on Fridays, Saturdays and Sundays, December being the busy period in the airline business. He'd agreed, which I was pleased about, as I thought it would give some normality back to his life; some structure and some social contact with people other than with hospital staff or patients.

Since the dreaded chemo had ceased, I had been regaining my strength with each passing day so I had thought I would drive myself in for radiation on those three occasions. Instead, my ever-reliable sister, Amanda, insisted on taking me on one of those days, and two dear friends made the offer to take me on the others. Jill, whom I had known for 24 years,

---

1. https://www.ncbi.nlm.nih.gov/pubmed/3308896

since we and our firstborn were both united at mother's group, was kind enough to volunteer for the hour-long drive each way. And the following Friday, for the very last session of radiotherapy, I was escorted by Philippa, who had become a good friend, even though the main reason for her being involved in our lives was in her role as Jon's occupational therapist in vocational training.

With a brain injury as severe as Jon's, there were many pieces that were required to fall into place in the matrix that manufactured his successful recovery. Family and community support were probably the most vital, along with enthusiasm, commitment, persistence and determination—not only from Jon, himself, but also from those who were involved in all aspects of the rehabilitation process. Philippa was integral to the part of the matrix which facilitated Jon's mainstream work and community participation. And, in my opinion, it is community participation, and not physical or cognitive recovery, that is the ultimate marker of a successful recovery.

'It's about time you let someone help you,' Jill had told me bluntly as she kissed me hello. 'It makes me feel like I'm doing something meaningful for you.' A sentiment echoed by others whom I slowly let into my private world of torment as the treatment began to near its end. I had never realised that you are actually giving a 'gift' by allowing someone to help you.

It was never intentional—actually that's codswallop, it was *very* intentional—for me to close myself off from the world, despite some very well-meaning and persistent friends. And, of course, I fear that in naming some I may miss others, so please indulge and forgive me for selecting just a few.

My dearest friend Esther—our friendship spans 40 years—is always the first person I call with news, good or bad—and the person I could sit next to and not say anything but feel comforted, our spirits are so akin. There are two very special ladies who came into my life as a result of reading *Paper Cranes*; both communicated which was far easier for me rather than making conversation. Dear Sylvia, who, along with her many emails and various gifts of love, knitted me several pairs of bed socks to keep my icy cold feet warm throughout the worst winter of my life. And the other was Ellen, whose weekly emails of encouragement found their way into my 'Inbox' from across the Pacific Ocean. Ellen's emails were like reading a satirical script written for a sitcom like *Seinfeld*—although about ordinary people she had met and their not-so-ordinary lives. She always brought a smile to my face with her 'momtras', and her anecdotal medical advice was priceless. She had first written to me in September 2008 after reading a copy of *Paper Cranes*. Her son, Brad, had worked on Jon as a physiotherapist at Epworth Rehabilitation Hospital in Melbourne, and had taken her a copy when he went back home to the USA.

Dear Cheryl,

Brad gave us your book *Paper Cranes* and I took it with me [on holidays]. Thank you so much for your inscription. I sat on the beach for four hours the first day and read the book almost more than halfway, and the next day I finished it within an hour or two. Needless to say, I cried basically through the entire book. I think I stopped crying at the point you wrote out your letter of your son's condition and accomplishments prior to his going back to school. That was around page 150 or so. It was a beautiful, heartfelt, inspirational piece of writing. I can honestly say I felt like I was right there with you all. You and your son made a huge impression on Brad. He learned so much working with your son and working with the people at Epworth this summer. I am so glad he was able to meet you and learn of your story.

So why did I hibernate for the better part of six months? One truth is that I didn't want sympathy, didn't want to talk about having cancer; I didn't know how to charitably receive well wishes for myself, or for that matter, any other kind of emotional support other than from the three people in my world to whom I was closest. The emotions I was feeling as a result of this illness were foreign to me, so how could I give a voice to them? My inner sanctum of private thoughts was profoundly affected. I don't mean my outlook on life or my values—those important priorities had been permanently adjusted after Jon's accident. Rather, it was my self-esteem that was altered, which in turn affected my ability to communicate with friends and colleagues who were kind enough to ring or visit. I appreciated every call, every card, every bunch of flowers, but I don't know if others appreciated that I didn't resemble myself and couldn't re-assemble myself, even temporarily, for a well-meaning chat.

Essentially, it was Rob who nourished me with his total love and selflessness whom I unashamedly relied upon. It was his strong arms that picked me up from where I'd fallen; his constant embrace from where I drew my strength. And it was him above all others whom I could never disappoint by *not* getting better.

'I don't know what I'd do without him. He's been so good to me!' I literally cried to Stephanie one afternoon as she set the table for the bountiful meal she had cooked for dinner. Stephanie and Steven lived about twenty minutes from us and at least twice a week would arrive with a piping hot meal. Nothing was, nor has ever been, too much trouble for them when it comes to being there for family. Without that kind of unconditional love and support, I know we would have struggled, and I can't imagine how families who are not as fortunate, endure.

'Cheryl, don't cry,' Stephanie said cradling me in her arms. 'He has been very, very good, we know that and are so proud of our son. But watching what *you* have been through, darling girl … I will never again complain.'

* * *

During November, I also had the opportunity to reschedule another one of the many public speaking commitments I had previously cancelled. Slipping into 'Emily' for the occasion, together with Rob as my dependable chauffeur, we first dropped Jon off at his warehouse job, and then made our way down the scenic coastal highway to the Illawarra region, a couple of hours south of Sydney. A spritely bunch of seniors appeared to enjoy my 30-minute talk about the importance of hope, and how we should never let anyone else's doubts blur our own vision (although I always feel somewhat impudent in remitting my own life lessons on those whose minds I am certain contain more wisdom than mine), and afterwards there was a brief question and answer session.

Without fail, as was the case at every talk I had done so far, I was asked about Chris and how he managed to turn out so well-adjusted.

'To be honest, I still have serious moments of maternal guilt at having to neglect Chris's needs for the best part of a decade, with all my energy being funnelled towards helping Jonathan reach his true potential. But it's funny how our kids learn through watching us in ways we don't realise or understand at the time. Last year when Chris was captain of his representative soccer team, and they were playing in their grand final, there were about two minutes left to play when the other team scored. Chris's team was down one-nil, and even Rob leant over to me and said, "We may as well go home—it's all over".

'Chris's teammates were obviously dejected, heads hanging low, as they carried the ball back to the centre circle for the final kick-off. Then one guy said, "It's over, Chris. Never mind, we did our best." Next minute Chris gathered his team in a circle around him, and from the centre of the field I could hear him yelling, "If any one of you thinks this game is over, get off the field now! Go on—go! Because it's not over until the final whistle blows."'

So they kicked off, and wouldn't you know it, they scored, which sent the match into extra time. His team scored twice more and won the grand final: three-one. I was so proud of him that day as the team hoisted him up on their shoulders after the match. Proud of his leadership and his actions, but mostly, proud, because I realised how much he had learned from quietly observing Rob and me with Jon these past

12 years. He'd learned that you never, ever give up, no matter what life hands you—you just keep going.'

'What are you writing now, Cheryl?' was the next question from a gentleman in the back row.

'I'm writing about some amazing post-World War II immigrants, the extreme life challenges they faced and overcame, including their daring tales of escape after the war. And what they brought with them to this country, both metaphorically and literally, in just one suitcase.'

'Have you ever been to your father's homeland?' A well-dressed lady asked (a question that would become part of nearly every Q & A at book talks down the track).

'Unfortunately, no,' came my reply, 'but I'm working on my husband to take me'.

'Where did you get your own inner strength from?' asked another member from the audience.

'I'm certainly not a psychologist nor a philosopher, but I do believe that we each possess a certain inner strength that sometimes only becomes evident when we are facing difficult challenges in our lives. However, speaking personally, my own inner strength was, and is, definitely influenced by both nature and nurture. I've had some amazing mentors in my life, two of whom I'm blessed to call my father and father-in-law.

Cheryl's maternal grandparents, with Pop on her christening day; with her Nana in the Loew backyard.

In the arms of her paternal grandparents, Anyu and Apu.

Cheryl, aged 4, standing in the front yard with her father's Vanguard in the background.

Cheryl (aged 15) and Robert (aged 19), 2 weeks after they met, 1975.

Cheryl and Rob's wedding – her father Fred, Cheryl, Rob and her mother, Joan, 1979.

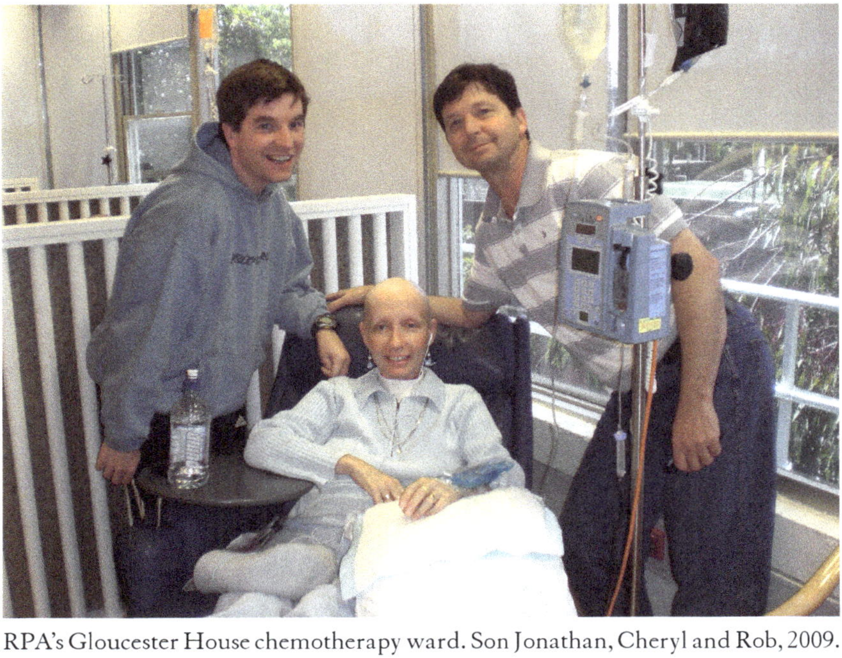

RPA's Gloucester House chemotherapy ward. Son Jonathan, Cheryl and Rob, 2009.

Celebrating Stephanie's birthday at Cheryl's home. From left: Jon, Cheryl, Chris, Stephanie and Steven, 2009.

Cheryl receives her Medal of the Order of Australia (OAM) from Governor Bashir. From left: Robert, Jonathan, Cheryl, Governor Bashir and Fred, 2014.

The magnificent Il Duomo
Cathedral, Florence, towers
over Jon and Rob, 2017.

Welcomed to Budapest, Hungary, by a splendorous moon shining over the Houses of Parliament, 2017.

A memorial with bullet holes from the 1956 Hungarian Revolution, Houses of Parliament, Budapest, 2017.

Rob, Jon and cousin Evelyn outside Rob's family home in Timişoara, 2017.

Rob and Jon at Rob's grandparents' grave, 2017.

Jon and Cheryl outside Cheryl's grandparents' home in the centre of Timişoara, Romania, 2017.

Cheryl and Rob's daughter-in-law, Danielle, holding Olivia (2 weeks old) with Chris holding Summer (19 months), 2017.

11

One step forward, two back

December 2009

Christmas came upon us with frantic last-minute shopping—so untypical of my usual performance with the pace and organisation of the festive season. I was quite exhausted from the radiotherapy which had only ended on December 14. Knowing my white cells were not multiplying as they should, putting me at risk of infection, so Rob and Chris went forth with lists in hand, amongst the crowds and the carols, to do my bidding. Jon's stash beneath the tinsel tree needed to be well-stocked if we were to be graced with his innocent wide-eyed expression of delight.

However, just like the first Christmas that family gathered after Jon's accident, this one held a slightly deeper and philosophical meaning for our extended family as we assembled at Steven and Stephanie's house for a feast of fine traditional fare. Raising glasses brimming with sparkling Moët, which Amanda supplied for the occasion, we toasted to the blessing of family and to everyone's future good health.

A few days later an ambulance was called to ferry me to our nearest hospital following my collapse with dehydration from a bad dose of gastroenteritis which I had probably caught on the plane trip to visit Dad in Melbourne earlier that week. Blood tests revealed my white cells were still well depleted. It was not a good way to bring in the new year of 2010.

Once back home, I was restless to find the necessary energy to participate in the activities which enhanced my life, giving it purpose and a feeling of contributing, rather than just observing life pass from the perimeters. I needed to *live* not just exist. Dismayed that I still became easily fatigued after venturing out or tackling more than one activity in a day, I began modestly, doing most of my voluntary committee work via teleconference and email.

Collaboration also began with Sarah Schoonwater from the CFMEU in the facilitation of the charity football match to be held in July. Together with the Canberra Raiders' marketing staff, we started designing a team jersey that would reflect the colours and logo of the not-for-profit organisation of my choosing. As the match was about raising awareness of acquired brain injury, naturally, I chose the relevant peak advocacy body: Brain Injury Australia (BIA).

Nick Rushworth, the BIA Executive Officer, was delighted to be on board and took over much of the liaising with the Canberra Raiders. Since 2004, Nick and I had been the only two consumer representatives on NSW Health's ACI Brain Injury Rehabilitation Directorate. From where I sat, no better advocate and policy influencer existed in the country. I always felt so privileged to call him both a friend and colleague.

Still, my restless mind felt a desperate need to keep busy, keep distracted. I went back to answering every email in my Inbox as soon as they appeared—saying 'yes' again to speaking engagements which would have taken me into the next six months. I began answering dozens of emotional emails from unknown carers desperately searching for help or direction. I also started working on Jon's rehabilitation activities again, though ironically, I found this more taxing on me than it was for him. I started reading, doing crosswords, taking longer strolls around the block. Cooking and writing, the two activities where I could lose myself to my imagination, once again became my salvation. It was my way of meditating; removing myself from this strange paradox of emotions I found myself within—at once overwhelmed with feelings of relief that treatment had ended, and surprised with my anxiety that it had indeed ended.

Realising I needed emotional support, I did what I knew would help, what I had advised so many others who wrote to me looking for help, to do—I sought out people who had walked this path before me. I knew support groups were a vital source of connectivity within the community. Support groups were a place where, through the sharing of similar stories, people could re-gain lost confidence thereby enabling them to trust in their decision-making capability. Through experience I understood that the significance of being connected to others often revealed itself during difficult times. However, declaring our loneliness or isolation can be tricky, as it can carry a perceived stigma. Admitting we are lonely can be like admitting we have failed in life's fundamental domains: belonging, love, attachment, well-being, and so forth. It flies in the face of our (or at least my own) basic instinct to put on a brave façade, which in turn makes it difficult to ask for help. I knew how to help others, but never realised how much strength you need to receive help.

Sadly, social separation, loneliness, isolation—whatever you wish to call it—is widespread. Unless recognised and treated, this can result in grim physical, mental and emotional consequences. Any way you look at it, being disconnected from other humans—especially those reading here who are dealing with similar life challenges—is bad for all of us. Life is a group effort. We can't do it alone. We need to take the journey with others.

Fortunately for me, there was one lunch in particular that Gail, my always effervescent neighbour, organised which helped me identify my thoughts. I met a lady there who had finished treatment for breast cancer a year earlier; she was able to relate to and label my feelings exactly—that you're walking a tight rope without a safety net. I also needed to be fed more stories of survival, so I hunted them out. It seems everyone knows someone with a negative cancer outcome and for some inexplicable reason they feel compelled to tell you of their friend's, mother's, sister's or cousin's relapse. It can easily become unproductive, and if you let it, can become a weighty pull towards negativity. I needed to hear how people moved forward with hope and optimism.

I had always been known for my optimistic outlook, but I guess sometimes, especially after traumatic episodes, it needs encouragement from other sources. Not long after my early PET scan remission, Professor Gibson had told me that he believed my good outcome was due to the combination of being blessed with the constant family support that he witnessed with Rob and Jon rarely leaving my side, and the positive attitude (or I think he may have called it 'stubbornness') I possessed.

Despite my positive outlook on life, however, I wouldn't be truthful if I didn't admit that as wonderful as it felt to be in remission, remission *per se* does not mean 'cured'. Naturally, the uncertainty evoked by occasional thoughts of a potential relapse, still brought with it questions regarding life and its transience. And, I was pragmatic enough to be fully cognisant that there was nothing special about me or my success; there were literally thousands of survivors out there. So, I decided to quietly ask around my network of friends. That's when I found some amazing mentors with positive outcomes who helped me enormously at this time.

12

Ubuntu a Nguni Bantu[1]
I am because we are

On 11 February 2010, I attended a meeting for the Agency for Clinical Innovation's Brain Injury Rehab Directorate. For the first time since being diagnosed on 12 June 2009, I was able to personally thank Maeve for beginning the chain of events that conspired in my recovery. Who knows what would have eventuated had she not rung me that evening, and then rung Kate Needham? (I had thanked Kate previously on the many occasions she kindly visited me at the RPA).

'Cheryl, you look so well,' Maeve said in her lovely Irish brogue.

'Thanks,' I replied. *Gosh I need to walk more, I'm so unfit,* I thought, catching my breath from the short flight of stairs.

Driving home, I felt a sense of satisfaction at being able to attend and maintain concentration during the long meeting, and it was good to see my colleagues with whom I had worked since 2004. By the time I left it was late, peak hour, and I hit traffic.

---

1. *Ubuntu* is a key theme in African philosophy that places an imperative on the importance of group or communal existence as opposed to the West's emphasis on individualism. As an aspect of African traditional philosophy, *Hunhu/Ubuntu* prides itself on the idea that the benefits and burdens of the community must be shared in such a way that no one is prejudiced. https://www.iep.utm.edu/hunhu/

'Ooh,' I uttered as I rubbed the heel of my hand into the centre of my chest, 'just a bit of pain. I must be overtired'.

After almost two hours in the car, I finally arrived home around seven and went to bed immediately, leaving Rob to take up the slack once again. Exhausted, I slept like a baby, but woke through the early hours of the morning with a familiar sharp and unrelenting chest pain. 'Shit! Not again,' I whispered into the darkness.

Allowing the morning peak-hour traffic to subside, after breakfast Rob drove me to the emergency department of the RPA where they took me in straight away, as they do anyone who presents with chest pain. After making sure my heart was ticking fine, they ordered plain X-rays, followed by a CT scan. Some hours later the treating doctor informed me that there were no signs of anything untoward on either scan.

'You won't find a blood clot of mine on a plain X-ray, nor a CT scan,' I offered. 'You need to do a VQ scan to rule it out.'

'Look, Cheryl,' the young doctor said, 'there's nothing showing in your blood tests and you've been given some pain medication which has reduced your pain, so I think it's safe to send you home'.

Not being one to argue, and definitely not wanting another admission, I got up as quickly as possible: 'Good, I'm out of here then'.

The chest pain intensified, as I suspected it would, and two days later I reluctantly rang Professor Gibson who told me to come into RPA immediately where he ordered a VQ scan. It showed I had not only one, but two pulmonary emboli.

Unashamedly, I cried like a little girl when they told me I was to be re-admitted to Ward 7 West 1. 'I just don't understand how that can happen when I'm already on blood thinning injections!' I said to anybody who would listen.

Another long week spent in my proverbial 'hotel suite' was broken by similar visits from worried family and anxious friends. One such visit was from treasured friend, Judy Keyes (née Pongrass). During her visit, Judy asked Jon, amongst other things, what his favourite food is.

'Schnitzel,' he replied. 'Mum makes the best schnitzel!'

She left with a promise to return with some Wiener Schnitzel, made the way she had been taught by her Hungarian mother, Clara. She fulfilled her pledge bringing enough schnitzel to feed a famine on the day of my discharge. Personally, I have never tasted better schnitzel before or since, but when Jon sent her a text message of thanks he wrote:

'Thank you for the schnitzel. It was excellent. Almost as good as my Mum's. I give you a nine out of ten.'

'Jon,' I said mortified, 'that wasn't exactly a nice way to say thank you'.

'I'm just being honest, Mum.' He replied in genuine sincerity.

Jeez, I must teach him to fib better, I thought, but just as quickly disregarded such judgment as his innocent truthfulness had to be one of his most endearing qualities.

Also, during that hospital stay, I had a call on my mobile from the secretary to Jodi McKay, the New South Wales' Minister for Women, asking if I would be available in March to make the opening address as the 2009 incumbent at the New South Wales Woman of the Year Award reception.

'Sure,' I said, realising by her tone that she didn't know I was unwell. 'I'd be honoured. What would you like me to speak about?'

'Oh, just about your year as 2009 Woman of the Year. What it meant to you and what you were able to achieve.'

'Um … I don't think you'd really like me to talk about that—' I began.

'Yes, Cheryl, that's exactly what we want you to do.'

'I don't think you understand. It hasn't been a great year for me in terms of health. I'm in hospital right now.'

'I see,' she replied. 'Then speak about what you're passionate about. That's, of course, if you're well enough to attend.'

'Oh, I'll be there, for sure,' I said, excited at the prospect of having the powerful ear of hundreds of politicians and leading community members.

*　*　*

A few days after arriving home, I answered a knock on the door, to find a tall, blonde attractive young woman, awkwardly holding a large cardboard box full of brightly coloured folded origami. I recognised the shape of the origami instantly—it was the symbol that had become renowned as our family emblem: the paper crane. In fact, on numerous occasions over the past few years I had been asked by total strangers, 'Are you the paper crane lady?'

The young woman, however, was not so easily recognisable. But when she introduced herself, I immediately remembered her name as one of Jon's old school friends from Aquinas College. She was one of many from his school year group that had made paper cranes and sent them into the Children's

Hospital with prayers and messages of hope—the very reason behind the title of my book about his recovery.

'Hi, Alana,' I said as I hugged her. 'It's great to see you. Come in, come in. What've you got there?'

'These are just some of the hundreds of paper cranes that our church and youth group have made for *you* this time. We heard on the grapevine that you have been unwell and we wanted to do something for you. There's more to come. I've set up a Facebook page with the name: "1000 paper cranes for Cheryl Koenig". I've also left a sign on a box at the church, asking people to pray for you and make paper cranes as they do—as a gesture for Lent.'

I was moved to tears by this kindness. To think she had organised so many people to pray for me, to even think of me, touched me beyond description.

In my opinion there is a special kind of energy that enters the universe from people connecting to people whether in real time or in thought. I was humbled to think that I was in the minds of so many compassionate people. Compassion, to me, is a deep-held belief that being inexplicably connected to each other by the very fact we are all human, makes us care about our fellow humans.

There are different levels of compassion, of course. Compassion and empathy are very different: empathy is what brings compassion alive. Empathy results when we truly understand what others have endured. Sadly, in my opinion, failure to empathise is a key part of societal problems today: crime, violence, war, racism, inequity—just to name a few. To be fully human you need empathy or else we risk polarisation.

As the daughter of a refugee, one of my particular concerns is the apathy around modern refugees and asylum seekers, especially in affluent countries. Still evident in many parts of the world is prejudice, racism and bigotry which has, unfortunately, gained its own momentum.

As I write the final draft of this book, in Christchurch, New Zealand, 50 peacefully praying people, including children, were gunned down in a mosque by a white supremacist, a fascist. The only consolable element about the whole tragic massacre came in the aftermath: in the truth, words and actions of the New Zealand Prime Minister, Jacinda Ardern. Her language embraced inclusion; her warmth, openness and personal dignity, portrayed empathy. And being the daughter of a persecuted people myself, Ardern embodies qualities I admire and aspire to and sincerely wish other national leaders would exemplify. If we don't each contribute towards an environment where violence *cannot* flourish, we will continue to be traumatised by this detrimental momentum currently bred by extremists. We will live in fear of life itself.

We need more stories, and individuals like Jacinda Ardern—to inspire us, to touch us, to move us. We should not remain indifferent to this world-wide problem that needs humane solutions. We need to imagine what it must be like to be persecuted because of our ethnicity, creed, or circumstance. To be nothing, belong nowhere, be voiceless in an indifferent world…

We must never stop trying. We must never lose hope for a better world.

'I am, because we are.'

13

My considered life

March 2010

March, with its milder days and easy autumn nights arrived, and before I realised, it was time to make that important speech at Parliament House. They had wanted to know about my year as 'Woman of the Year', and it was during those ten tedious days in hospital in February when I had plenty of time, that I formulated exactly what I would speak about. Twelve months earlier when I had accepted the award, I had done so on behalf of all women carers, so it didn't take me long to work out that carers would once again be the focus of my speech. I decided to speak about the recent research that proved that compared with other demographics, a higher percentage of carers suffered from chronic illness and pain. I decided to use myself as an example.[1]

My hair had slowly begun to grow back; it was about half a centimetre long and a mixture of grey and black curls; nothing like the hair that had abandoned me, but I didn't care: hair of any description was a bonus. However, to get the point of my speech across with more emphasis, I decided not to wear 'Emily', but instead go *au naturel*.

Rob and Jon accompanied me to the cocktail reception where we were seated in the front row next to the Minister

---

1. Deakin University, Australian Unity, CarersAust, 2007.

for Health, Carmel Tebbutt, who was filling in for the new premier, Kristina Keneally (whose son had broken his arm at school only hours before the event).

Earlier in the day I'd felt some apprehension at the prospect of sharing the last 12 months of my life, with its trials and tribulations, in front of so many people. *After chemotherapy, everything else should be a walk in the park,* I'd told myself to overcome my fearfulness. But in actuality, I only had to think of Jon for inspiration, for courage. Courage doesn't have to be a big and bold capital 'C'; it can be an enduring courage that begins with a small 'c'. Because, despite living in a society that values status, production and competition, the boy who was once top of his class academically, with an exceptional talent in all things musical and who could run like the wind had, through *his* enduring courage, demonstrated that personal credibility doesn't come in the form of IQ numbers, degrees or sporting trophies. Not only had Jon learnt to live with his residual impairments but, importantly, he had taught those around him to do the same. My amazing son had given me the gift of understanding the substance of small pleasures, of considering things in a more meaningful way, of leading a more 'considered' life. Minor things that were once taken for granted were now the palette from which our family added richness and colour to our lives. Jon's endurance has enabled us to take pleasure in the richness of the ordinary experience.

Being a relatively short speech of ten minutes, I had memorised most of it and, despite talking about the insidious nature of cancer and its implications for the lives of families (especially if they were 'carer-families'), I held my composure and spoke with as much clarity and feeling as I could. Whilst speaking, when I cast a glance at my two most loyal supporters, Rob and Jon, they were both sending me silent acknowledgment that I was going well: Rob with a slight nodding of his head, and Jon smiling proudly up at me.

Towards the end of the speech, however, I couldn't look in their direction as I sensed Rob had tears threatening to spill, and I knew only too well how I would respond to his emotional expression.

Afterwards I was amazed when at least six people asked for a copy of the speech. I was also asked to speak at two other functions further into the year, and the line-up of people to speak with me at the conclusion of the formal proceedings was truly humbling. A copy of most of my speech was actually recorded in *Hansard* by Alison Megarrity, our local member of parliament, who delivered a Private Member's Statement about the evening.

NSW LEGISLATIVE ASSEMBLY
PRIVATE MEMBERS STATEMENT
ALISON MEGARRITY MP
16 MARCH 2010
NSW WOMAN OF THE YEAR AWARDS

Ms ALISON MEGARRITY (Menai) [1.05 p.m.]: Last week the 2010 New South Wales' Woman of the Year event was held in Parliament House. The Menai electorate nominee was Melinda Cruz. Melinda is the founder and chief executive officer of the Miracle Babies Foundation. This charity raises about $500,000 each year for equipment and resources to assist premature and sick babies. It also provides practical and emotional support for families throughout Australia during their journey through a newborn intensive care unit, the transition to home and onwards. In nominating Melinda, I said that her initiative in founding and remaining so committed to the development of an organisation that has supported so many families in my electorate and well beyond it was an inspiration. It was a pleasure to welcome Melinda and her husband, Chris, to the event last week. They are clearly loving and devoted parents to sons Elijah, 7, Dillon, 5, and Jasper, 3.

The keynote speaker on the night was Cheryl Koenig, the 2009 Menai electorate and overall New South Wales Woman of the Year. Cheryl acknowledged the inspiring role many women play in promoting a socially just, and thereby cohesive, community. It is her belief that the most crucial investment we can make as individuals is in our shared social well-being. She said that it was therefore very reassuring to see a Premier and a Government that also shared this principle. Cheryl reminded us that she had accepted the 2009 award on behalf of all New South Wales women Carers for the contribution they make every single day.

In her trademark honest approach, she also explained that only eight weeks after last year's event her world came crashing down when she was diagnosed with a life-threatening blood cancer. The good news is that she is now in remission, but she wanted to highlight the frequency with which she had noticed that Carers suffer illness themselves. In fact, her observations are backed up by Australia's only female Nobel Prize winner, Dr Elizabeth Blackburn, who found that people who live with chronic stress, such as those who are the primary caregivers of dementia patients or children with a disability, are more prone to serious disease. I would like to provide the House with a substantial quote from Cheryl's speech that night. Unfortunately, it will not be the same as hearing Cheryl deliver these words straight from her heart, but

I think by the conclusion everyone will agree that her advice deserves the widest possible audience. She said:

> 'Every experience in life should teach us something. So what life lessons did I learn from 2009? Well, firstly I learnt that when you sit in a chemo ward with toxins roping your veins and stripping away, drip by drip, the very essence of who you once were, it matters little what 'title' you carry or what letters stand before or after your name. What truly matters is, of course, the love of your family and the very precious time you have to spend with them. I also learnt that even though we can't always define our own destiny, as sometimes, when we least expect it, 'life' can get in our way, what we can do is define our own quality of life, and this is now my message at my talks to Carers and people with disability. Even when faced with life's hardest challenges, you can choose how you respond to your suffering—you can let it be your undoing, or you can choose to create meaning and purpose from adversity. As the philosopher Socrates said: "The really valuable life is the considered life". Which signifies to me that we really need to be thoughtful about what we do. As women, we play an integral role in shaping our home environments, communities, places of work—including boardrooms and governments—so I encourage you all to really think about what it is you truly value, what you're aiming for, and how your own 'considered life' contributes towards a more humane and caring society.'

I only wish that I had time today to have every word of Cheryl's speech recorded in Hansard because from where I was sitting, I could tell that her speech touched every person there that night. As the Minister for Women said, upon resuming the microphone, no one was in any doubt as to why Cheryl was last year's overall winner.

Later that night I happened to see television coverage of the Academy Awards held the same day. The celebrity-filled audience jumped up to provide a standing ovation to virtually every second award winner. I recalled and regretted that I had earlier resisted an overwhelming urge to do the very same thing as Cheryl finished her address. Had I done so I believe that every member of our more typically restrained Australian audience would have quickly followed in a fitting tribute. In my capacity as the member for Menai I am fortunate to know Cheryl's whole family. So, I put on record that my ovation would have honoured also Cheryl's wonderful husband Robert and sons Christopher and Jonathan.

I join with other members of the House in congratulating every 2010 Woman of the Year nominee and I feel sure that all members join me in wishing the whole Koenig family continued health and happiness.

14

We all fall down

Another reality check brought me back down to earth a few weeks later as April saw me re-admitted to the RPA with yet a new hurdle to face and overcome. This time it was a potentially serious complication from radiation to the neck, called post-radiation myelitis, or inflammation of the nerves in the spinal cord. It gave a weird sensation that felt a bit like having your mobile phone on vibrate in your pocket—only the vibration started at the waist and travelled down both my legs to my toes. The experience worsened with physical exertion; and, oddly, whenever I bent my head forward (or flexed my neck) a sensation like an electric shock travelled down my legs. Painless, but disconcerting.

'It's okay,' I said to Rob when we found out it would probably be permanent. 'As long as it's not painful, I can live with it.'

It would give me no end of pleasure to be able to state that this unusual medical phenomenon would be the last health complication I would face, but there were still more awaiting me—and painful too, just to test me further!

* * *

July rolled around and brought with its cooler days one of the highlights of Jon's life. With everything in place for the big charity match to raise awareness of brain injury—including a specially designed jersey with the colours and logo of Brain Injury Australia, which would be auctioned off after the game with funds donated to BIA and live national television coverage of the match through *Foxtel*—Jon was asked to run (yes, run!) the Canberra Raiders Football team onto the field. The whole family, including Steven, Stephanie and Chris's delightful new girlfriend, Danielle, were accommodated by the CFMEU/Tradies Club at their affiliated hotel, and were treated to dinner in their corporate box.

Nick Rushworth also attended and gave an articulate and informed half-time interview in front of a crowd of more than 10,000 spectators, about brain injury, in general. I was then asked questions about the personal effect ABI had on families. The star of the show was the young man himself, though. Never have I been prouder of him! The astute and often humorous way he answered questions thrown at him randomly from every corner; the way he didn't get nervous with a TV film crew from the ABC following him around that day—and, indeed, the previous week at his various jobs—and the way he performed his best run to date, perfectly, for the occasion. Even Gavin Williams, the senior neurophysiotherapist from Epworth Rehabilitation Hospital in Melbourne (who is not one to be easily impressed) sent an email saying what a great run he managed to pull off. It was an evening, an event, to remember, by all who attended.

Recognition and credit must also be given to the Canberra Raiders players, who interacted with Jon so brilliantly in the dressing room before, during and especially after the match they won. Later seeing footage of him chanting the team song with all the strapping young players patting him on the back, was absolutely priceless!

When he returned to the corporate box at the end of the game, I said to him in jest: 'I saw you with all those cheer girls. I noticed your wily grin; I think that was your favourite part of the night!'

'Come on, Mum … No need to get personal!' he replied, smiling.

The following week, the ABC *7.30 Report* depicted a week in the life of Jono called, 'New Hope for Brain Injured', which portrayed how hard he had worked to be integrated within society again. It also gave a snapshot of new medical evidence about brain repair.

So much awareness was generated from that football match and subsequent television program. A rival television channel asked us to come in for a live chat about Jon's extraordinary achievements on their *Sunrise* program. My website went into meltdown with dozens of emails seeking advice or direction. For weeks and months afterwards, people stopped us in the shops or in the street just to say, 'Good on you, Jono'.

It gave me immense pride to know I had contributed in a small way to reducing the social stigma by challenging the stereotyping attached to acquired brain injury. Later in the year I was fortunate enough to receive the rare honour of being made a Lifetime Member of Brain Injury Association of New South Wales for: 'Outstanding contributions to the awareness of brain injury'.

No one, except for family members and Professor Gibson, knew that exactly a week before the big charity match, I went to bed one night feeling fine, only to wake up in the early hours of the morning with severe and sudden onset of bone and joint pain. So extreme was the pain that I was literally unable to move and had no choice but to ring Professor Gibson a few days later when the pain moved into my chest.

'You've got to help me,' I said, in desperation. 'I've got to be in Canberra in four days' time for the big match; plus I have raffles and other fundraising things to organise, and I've got this blasted chest pain.'

'Any other symptoms?'

'When I walk it feels as if I'm walking on broken glass, my finger joints are so sore and swollen I can't get my rings off, and I can't even lift my arms above my shoulders!'

'Okay,' he replied, 'I know if Cheryl Koenig's telling me it's bad, then it has to be *really* bad. Have you got some Prednisone tablets left at home?'

'Yes'.

'I want you to take 25 milligrams for the next week, then come and see me when you get back home.'

The Prednisone did its thing and I was able to move around a little more freely. Yet despite the pain still making itself felt during the extremely busy weekend in Canberra, I was determined not to let it dampen the occasion, both for Jon's sake, and for the important agenda and people we were representing.

It took several months of investigative tests to be able to produce a name for this most disabling setback: Sjogren's disease—an auto-immune disease that features the abnormally high production of antibodies in the blood that are directed against various tissues of the body (cells destroying cells, basically), sometimes producing, amongst other symptoms, an inflammatory arthritic condition in the bones and joints. In my case it may have been triggered either by my cancer of the immune or lymphatic system, or by the treatment itself. And, as my mother had rheumatoid arthritis, I may have had a pre-disposition to the disease, just waiting for a trigger. It has definitely been a hard one for me to get my head around— mainly because it was initially painful and restrictive. But at least it's not life-threatening, and so I know what I must do: keep moving, keep busy, and just handle it.

* * *

At the end of 2010, I applied, was interviewed and successfully appointed as a council member on the inaugural New South Wales Carers Advisory Council. Eleven carers from diverse backgrounds, plus three people from carer advocate organisations, made up the Council whose role was to advance the interests of carers in NSW by providing advice to the Minister for Ageing and Disability Services and the Office for Carers on legislation, policy, and matters that have a significant impact on the lives of over 850,000 carers across NSW.

'Not another committee, Chez!' Rob groaned.

'Service to others is the rent you pay for your time here on earth—or something like that,' I replied, using one of my favourite quotes from Muhammed Ali.

Rob just shook his head, so I tried for another famous quote: 'My work is my life,' as Jon said to an MP one day, who later quoted him in *Hansard*—which does makes him famous in a way. Jon was speaking his absolute truth, though: he definitely does live for every one of his five part-time jobs.

'But you're doing too much, honey. You still get so tired.'

He was right, of course—my body was still a battleground. However, I felt that what he didn't understand is that I had lost faith in idle talk and gestures from government bodies. I was always telling others, 'if the culture doesn't work, don't buy it'. With this opportunity, I hoped to continue to validate my ethical compass through giving time to advocate on behalf of carers in an effort to improve government policy and services. As carers, we had made some progress with recognition and validation, but there was still so much more work to be done to improve services.

From my experience thus far on government committees, there was often duplication, or waste of funds, overlap and under-utilisation of existing good local resources. There had been good headway in some areas, and there had been average or non-existent headway in other areas. From my personal perspective, if we don't care enough to get involved, to use our voices to drive change, then we basically can't complain when things remain static.

For to give, is to want more, isn't it? Of course, there's considered and ill-considered giving, as well as different motivations for giving. I have never wanted recognition—my name on a building, for example. Rather, my desire is driven by the want of a better quality of life for carers, people with disability and other marginalised sectors. It's easy to forget that at the heart of giving is compassion. Giving is what makes me feel good. Not my car, my house, not how I look. When I give my time, it's as close as I get to feeling healthy, feeling good about *me*.

I believe the way to get meaning in life is to devote yourself to caring about others. Devote yourself to community. Devote yourself to creating something that gives purpose to your life. I've learnt to give not because I have much to offer, but because I understand what it is to need help.

15

The imposters of triumph and disaster

Two major events happened for Jon at the start of 2011. The first was him finally being able to purchase the new car he had dreamt about, longed for, saved for, and nagged us constantly for, over so many years—ever since his younger brother had bought himself a car some six years earlier (proving sibling rivalry never really ceases!).

It was a marvellous feat for him and I was elated to have seen one of his many dreams for the future fulfilled. The second, and equally significant, was the start of a new job as a junior office administration clerk with the law firm, Slater and Gordon. Many corporations promote themselves as being an equal opportunity employer, but until they hire people with a disability, they sadly fall short of the mark, and will never truly experience the very real benefits to be had by both employee and employer.

Shortly after Jon's commencement, Michael Lawandi, a senior solicitor in the firm, released a media statement which said that Jonathan was a real asset to the firm. He went on to say: 'Jonathan is an incredibly valuable addition to our staff. He is an independent worker who fits in well with our team and clients.' Although he needs support for some clerical tasks, given his unsteady right hand and hemiplegic left, nothing is ever too much trouble for the wonderful office manager Maria, another angel in our lives. She insists he adds to her day just by his charming, funny and cheeky presence.

And the warehouse manager at J.B. Metropolitan Distributors where Jon works two days a week on the end of a production line, expressed similar sentiments after many weeks of my thanking him profusely for the opportunity and assistance he provided Jon. 'Cheryl, you have to stop thanking us. It's we who should be thanking you—thanking you for bringing Jon into work. Since he started here, we've had fewer employee sick days, fewer complaints of headaches and other trivialities. The employees see how hard Jon tries with his limited arm function, and how he goes about his day with such a happy disposition, and it's a reality check for them.'

You see, people with disability are just like anyone else when it comes to how they feel about working and contributing to society. And just like everyone else, it's not until we are without work that we recognise how much structure, identity and self-esteem employment provides. Jon is so fortunate to have people willing to assist him in his various jobs. Daphne and Janice, who support Jon on Mondays at Sutherland Shire Council, are invaluable.

Slater and Gordon Lawyers, J.B. Metropolitan Distributors and Sutherland Shire Council have shown themselves to be humane and caring workplaces, that place people above profit. As a family, we feel blessed that each have given Jonathan a fantastic opportunity.

* * *

Hard as I tried to stay actively engaged in the community, advocating on behalf of carers and people with disability, as

2012 progressed I knew my health was slowly declining. My mobility was worsening due to a subtly progressive weakening of my legs, which also involved an aggravation of pain in standing or walking up hills or stairs or, in fact, a distance of more than 200 metres. And then I had a worsening of the unsettling vibrating sensation (which first began in my legs), throwing a spanner in the works. For now, it had traversed up my body to about chest level.

When 'the whole-of-torso-tremor' first happened, I remember asking Rob if the bed or room was shaking—like an earth tremor. That's how weird and strong a sensation it felt. It's made worse by physical activity, so if I do too much—oh, like walk up a small hill—I shake and sometimes, even stumble. I now have a loss of sensation from T2 down (thoracic spine, level two, or equivalent to chest level) affecting my bladder, bowel, balance and possibly a few other 'b' words I could throw in! They have a name for it—transverse myelitis—and if you research it, it sounds damn scary. I refuse to give in, however. The main thing to focus on, I tell myself, is that I'm still in remission from cancer, the rest is just 'stuff' that I have to learn to adjust to and adapt my life around.

It was 2013—a magical year. A Koenig family wedding year. Aged 26, my silent achiever, my unassuming, sweet son, Chris, spread his wings and married the girl of his dreams: the vivacious, delightful Danielle. From the outset, Danielle included me in nearly all of her ideas and preparations, for which I was so grateful. Firstly, it began with a day in the city to look at bridal gowns with her mum, Leanne, her sister Jenna, and best friend, Haylee (her youngest sister, also named Haylee, was living in England and due home one month before the wedding). With a swag of pills to keep me on my feet, I managed to trail from shop to shop, enjoying every single minute.

So caught up was I in the enchantment of their upcoming nuptials, I decided to give my beautiful daughter-in-law to-be a bridal shower. 'Impossible', 'You can't', or 'No way', said well-meaning friends and family to the idea of me hosting nearly 30 ladies for a high tea at home. But as Rob had come to know so well, the more you tell me 'can't', the more determined it makes me to do the opposite. (Perhaps Jon is more like me than I realised!) So, with lots of assistance from Danielle's mum and sister, the afternoon was a fabulous success and prelude into what can only be described as our unforgettable year of happiness.

On October 26, Chris married his sweetheart in Bowral, located in the Southern Highlands of New South Wales. We had a lovely weekend of festivities which culminated in a fairy-tale garden ceremony. Everything was as close to perfection as could possibly be: from Danielle herself—no more gorgeous bride could ever exist, in her strapless ivory gown with encrusted diamante bodice; to the electric blue chiffon of the beautiful bridesmaids as they floated across the manicured lawns; to my dashing sons who stood in-waiting together, under a canopy of luminous green foliage.

Chris, whom I've never seen smile more than he did that day, with Jon his best man (both ritually and literally) by his side—where he belonged, belongs—his eyes shining with pride, with a grin to match.

* * *

Since 2010, each Australia Day I have been given the amazing honour of being an Australia Day Ambassador. This involves travelling to regional parts of New South Wales to deliver an Australia Day address on what it means to be Australian (or something to that effect) as well as present local citizens with community awards. Rob and Jon travel with me, naturally, and the welcome and hospitality of the wonderful townsfolk from places such as Dunedoo, Coolah, Menora, Boorowa, Griffith, Marulan, Goulburn, Blayney, Cowra, Shoalhaven and Wingecarribbe Shires, along with meeting inspiring people who have achieved much within their communities, has indeed been one of the highlights of each year.

In preparing my first ambassador's address in 2010 for our visit to the town of Dunedoo in the beautiful Warrumbungle Shire, I asked my family if they could think of any typically Australian vernacular that I used.

'Well,' Chris replied, 'you often say: "Fair dinkum, you're a bloody idiot", you know, when people do something stupid'.

'I do not!'

'Yep, you do. But if you don't want to say that, you also say "bloody oath" a fair bit.'

So 'bloody oath' made the script, and I hope I haven't shocked too many people using that term in every town I have since visited.

* * *

Seasons swept by and time, like a thief, robbed me of an effortless and pain-free life. Sleep was becoming a permanent stranger. Somehow, I managed to push on with my brave façade—doing what was important to the essence of my being. My happiness and sense of moral duty, I guess, go hand in hand.

When I became unable to use public transport due to the tremors or pain affecting my mobility, the kind Secretariat from the NSW' Carers Advisory Council, sent private transport to enable my attendance at meetings. Very reluctantly, I was forced to say goodbye to most of my other committee work, as driving out of my local area had also become an issue.

However, I still answered every single email that graced my Inbox—especially if it was from other carers or people with disability who needed direction or support: 'kindness costs nothing,' as my mum was fond of saying.

The reward of that small effort made itself known to me one idle morning, like a freight train roaring through a sleepy village. Over the proceeding months, several email communiques back and forth took place between me and an obviously stressed carer. That morning, however, before I began work on my manuscript or attended to any other email enquiries, something compelled me to check in with this lady.

'Hi, Julie,' I wrote. *'Just thinking of you this morning and wondering how you are going?'* Nothing more. That simple.

Some minutes later she replied: *'Hi, Cheryl. Thanks for asking. I was just sitting here thinking about how I would top myself, until your email arrived. It made me realise someone out there actually cares.'*

* * *

In January 2014, something very special occurred … I was named in the Australia Day Honours List to receive a Medal in the Order of Australia (OAM), one of our country's highest awards: *'For services to people with disabilities, their carers and families'*. It's not often that I am speechless (just ask Rob), but seriously, what adjectives are there to describe the privilege of being the recipient of such a prestigious award? Yet, I really thought that this award more aptly belonged to Rob—he deserved the medal for everything he does for me and Jon. We would not have survived a day without him.

My dad flew up from Melbourne for the presentation by Governor Marie Bashir at Government House. I wore the same mother-of-the-groom outfit for which I had paid a bomb months earlier. Before being seated in an elegant hall within Government House, the 50 or so recipients were given a rundown on protocol: when to stand; where to line up and wait for your name and biography to be read out; when to enter; how far from the Governor to stop, to stand and shake hands, etcetera. We were also given a choice of whether to bow or curtsey before the official handshake.

'I think I'll curtsey,' I said to the woman behind me in the queue, as we inched closer to the mark indicating where we should stand before entering. 'I mean, how often in life does one get the chance to curtsey?'

'I'm going to bow,' she replied. 'My heels are too high for a curtsey; I'm so nervous I'd probably fall.'

Bloody oath! I didn't feel nervous until she said that. And when my turn came, I mucked the whole damn thing up. I waltzed in and didn't stop the one metre required before either bowing or curtseying. Instead I shook the Governor's hand first, then stepped back and performed some sort of half-bow-half-curtsey thing. She didn't seem to mind though. She took my hand, smiled and whispered: 'Out of everyone here, your work for carers and the disabled is the most important'.

'Thank you, Governor.'

'And by the way … I just adore your outfit. Where did you get it?'

Walking away, I glanced over at my proud fan club: Rob, Jon and Dad, clasping my grandmother, Anyu's, one-metre-long rope chain that I had twisted twice around my neck. I had just finished writing about this priceless heirloom left to Dad by his mother in *With Just One Suitcase*. It was purchased in Venice nearly 100 years ago by my grandfather. So, as I held it gently, smiled to my men and proudly walked down the aisle with my medal of honour pinned on, I felt sure Anyu, and Mum, would have been equally proud of me that day.

16

More lucky than gifted

During 2014, through research into the book industry, I was fortunate to discover a new publisher who believed in the preservation of the kaleidoscope of tales that make up the rich tapestry of Australia today. I was impressed with Wild Dingo Press's backlist of books, as well as their vision statement which I shared, including, 'shedding light on social issues' and 'sharing the rich cultural output and traditions of those oft-discussed but denied a voice…'

These statements actually played a significant role in compelling me to take on this project, as rarely do refugees (from past or present eras) have the opportunity of recounting their epic land or sea voyages. Of trudging across horizons with little else but hope packed in just one suitcase. Many suppress their fascinating and courageous stories often because of their overwhelming need to forget … to bury the past and rebuild their aborted lives.

But whatever our ancestral history, to remind ourselves of the link with our origins is often how we can best prepare for the future. It is where, if we look back, we may find some of the best examples of trusting in the power of hope; trusting in the importance of visualising how circumstances can change with great desire and determination—just like my two fathers and the many thousands of people who found themselves displaced after World War II. And despite *With Just One*

Suitcase being an historical memoir there was also no escaping my thoughts that a story like this was still a topical issue in the world today. People smugglers matched up with desperate refugees who have sold everything they own to buy themselves passage are, unfortunately, contemporaneous themes.

As I delved into my patriarchs' characteristics of valour, daring and imagination, I realised that these formed only part of the mosaic which combined to create a successful representation of life, not only for them, but for the many refugees who have sought a haven on our sandy shores. Hope proved of equal importance. Hope created aspirations, a faithfulness to keep hold of a dream, and through tenacity, eventual accomplishment. And even though sometimes I felt my own sense of hope riddled with despair—as if I was trundled along on a journey from which there was no getting off—there were many inspiring teachings to heed from my mentors. Indeed, from all those who survived and continue to survive displacement and marginalisation.

*   *   *

On 19 June 2015, after some insightful editing from Catherine Lewis and Iris Breuer from Wild Dingo Press, *With Just One Suitcase* was finally launched. Just as I had done in 2008 with the launch of *Paper Cranes,* I wanted to organise a fundraising gala dinner. The proceeds raised would be donated to an organisation for whom I was proud to be an ambassador and would in 2016, become a Life Member of: the Sutherland Shire Carer Support Service (SSCSS).

Plans were going as well as they could organising what was to be a huge event with only three months' preparation time. As always, there were the naysayers: 'Can't be done', 'Not enough time for such grand ideas', they said. But by now, dear reader, you will have come to understand that those words are like oxygen to a fire. So, despite another health setback with a shocking dose of shingles which confined me to bed for two weeks and even an overnight stay in hospital with possible encephalitis, I pressed on as best I could in garnishing raffle prizes and corporate sponsors. But the rash and associated nerve pain was indeed nasty. It first appeared on my left buttock (making it difficult to even lie on my bum in bed) then travelled down the length of my sciatic nerve. And, just as the neurologist predicted, due to my weakened immune system, I would get the blasted infliction again.

However, nearly 300 guests attended the gala and, with the sterling help from Tracy, Leonie and the small team from SSCSS, it was a fabulous night. We raised over $18,500 which was used to run resilience courses for carers.

With the evolving political landscape in the disability arena, community organisations such as SSCSS were facing slashed government funding, the logic being to replace existing local services with regional hubs, national websites and 1800 numbers. SSCSS, however, is more than 'just' a community service. To have a better understanding of the value a community service organisation brings to an area, you also need to look beyond service delivery. Over the last 20 years, through the combined direction, advocacy, support groups and extensive range of service programs SSCSS provide, carers in our community have the opportunity to participate in life through various activities of choice. And choice is important.

Never underestimate the power of having choice and control in life, no matter what that life looks like. In addition, SSCSS has developed and nurtured invaluable networks and infrastructure within the community.

Underpinning all this is what these types of community-based organisations also do to promote a sense of well-being amongst carers. And well-being is more than the absence of ill-health; it is much more than the state of being well. It is about affirmative personal experiences: that is, a feeling that you can achieve something positive or have a sense of purpose in life. Well-being encompasses experiences such as quality of life, contentment, happiness, a sense of inclusiveness and even prosperity.

When governments and local organisations provide comprehensive opportunities to participate in the community to all sectors of society (but especially the marginalised, such as people with disability, carers, refugees and the homeless), they are in fact, fostering societal inclusion. Why is that important? Because a socially inclusive community is one— in simple terms—where everyone can enjoy the opportunity of participation, be it in recreational or cultural activities or learning new skills. It's where more people are 'one of us' rather than an excluded, 'one of them'.

* * *

Following on from the launch of the book, the next few months of my life became extraordinarily busy (or even busier than usual!) with book promotions and media interviews. Dad and Rob's dad, Steven—my 84 and 87-year-old reluctant heroes—became celebrities of a kind. Their stories touched and inspired many people who wrote to me after hearing them interviewed on radio or reading about them. If I could capture my favourite reviews and 'fan mail' in just a couple of instances, it would be these:

Cheryl Koenig is to be congratulated. She has written a masterpiece. With great skill Cheryl has written an immensely readable, gripping biography documenting daily life in a crazed world. The story begins with a thumbnail sketch of life in semi-rural Romania at the outbreak of the second world war and moves on to relate the experiences, in that country, of her then youthful father and father-in-law. Many years later, in Sydney, Australia, they chance to be reunited when Cheryl nervously introduces her father to the father of her future husband.

The writing is powerful, in the first person, giving the reader a fly-on-the-wall feeling of being there. Having thoroughly researched the period Cheryl is able to construe the hitherto unknown Romanian perspective with great credibility, and, as if they hadn't already suffered enough, she goes on to relate how these amazing young men had the courage and strength to take flight and start a new life in this far flung land. That they survived at all is a miracle.

—Lucky Duck, Sydney[1]

And this short email captured the book's thematic essence:

Hi Cheryl

Just wanted to let you know how much I enjoyed your book. Our generation have had it so easy in comparison to the ones before us, haven't we? When you hear the stories of what some people had to endure during those who horrible times of war and yet still manage to go on to achieve so much out of life, in a new country, with virtually

---

1. Source: https://www.booktopia.com.au/with-just-one-suitcase-cheryl-koenig/prod9780987178589.html

nothing, is inspirational. And what an amazing turn of events to meet up and become connected in such a way so many years later … they say truth is stranger than fiction!

Thank you for sharing their/your story with us.

Regards,

J.K.

* * *

Four months before the book launch, when the idea was but a small seed germinating in my mind, I rang my good friend, Glenn Wheeler, to see if he would give his time to MC this event, as he had done in 2008 for *Paper Cranes*.

'Just name the date, Cheryl, and I'm there.' The busy but ever-generous media man replied.

Little did either of us know that his unstinting commitment to assist the fundraiser could well have been our last conversation. Four days later, whilst riding his motor scooter on a peaceful weekend not far from his family home in the southern suburbs of Sydney, a devastating and life-changing incident occurred: he was struck down by a reckless driver. He sustained a traumatic brain injury—similar in many ways to Jon's—surviving against the odds and is in the process of extensive rehabilitation.

Glenn had been a huge supporter of brain injury awareness. Indeed, we first crossed paths in 2006 when he was the MC at a fundraiser for Liverpool Brain Injury Unit—ironically the place he would end up spending one year of his life.

In August 2016, I was given the great privilege of being asked to speak at a fundraiser to help support Glenn's ongoing rehabilitation requirements.

Wheeler's Late Lunch
26 June 2016

It's an absolute honour to be standing here today to say a few words about my, and everyone's mate, Glenn! I've spoken all around the country, the other side of the world, in fact, in front of doctors, politicians, academics and the like. And truth be told, this speech means more to me than any other.

That's because of the inspirational guy about whom I'll be speaking.

But first a bit of our family background—as I'm sure most of you are wondering: 'who the bloody hell is this strange woman?' There's nothing special about me. There is, however, something special about my son, Jono, and Glenn's friendship.

Glenn entered our family's life over ten years ago, before the release of my third book Paper Cranes. And just as Glenn has done hundreds of times for hundreds of people and hundreds of charities, he was the MC at a couple of charity events that I had organised to (ironically) raise money for people with acquired brain injury.

Glenn made friends instantly with my then 21-year-old son, Jono, and as outlined in my book, Glenn came to Jono's rescue when he was unfairly dismissed from his workplace. Glenn's been a regular visitor at the Koenig household to share a beer and cheese platter with his mate (and us, Jono's parents) ever since. And Jono's been a regular pain-in-the-butt probably killing off Glenn's radio audience with his crappy jokes, following every serious interview I've done on-air with Glenn over important carer issues.

What's so special about their relationship? Well, you see Jono, who's here today, was only 12 when he was hit by a speeding car and sent some 20 metres through the air. It happened 100 metres from our family home, on a quiet suburban street, on a weekend.

I was on the scene within minutes and he actually died in my arms on the road before being revived by paramedics. On the way to hospital things deteriorated again and with the ambulance stopped for 20 minutes in the middle of busy Forest Road in Peakhurst, they brought him back to life.

At St George Hospital, we were told not to expect him to survive the night. And when he did miraculously pull through, we were told the same thing every night for the next three weeks in the intensive care unit of the Children's Hospital. He was in a coma for months and sustained the worst traumatic brain injury one doctor told us he had ever seen.

In fact, we were told to turn off life support. Told that if he survived, he would remain in a persistent vegetative state; told he'd never walk, talk or eat again. Well, we weren't going to settle for that, were we? Stubborn, you say? Yep! Just like my mate GW and his family ... my bloody oath!

No one was going to tell me what my son's potential was going to be. So, Team Jono set to work, and for the next decade we worked on him around the clock. It took blood, sweat and tears (and some alcohol, at times!), but as of today, Jono can not only walk, but run, ski, play tennis, play piano, drive—as well as work five days a week in four mainstream part-time jobs.

But this isn't Jono's story, nor Jono's day (Lord knows he's had enough of the limelight to last a lifetime! His head is so big, he can hardly fit through a doorway!). I'm just telling you this as a way of showing who we are, what Glenn means to our family, and the stupid, reckless irony of destiny!

For today is Glenn's day to shine—just like the star he's always been. In fact, right from the early days following that totally irresponsible and devastating incident—as news of Glenn's injuries seeped through—I sensed that he would be all right.

You see, I know the characteristics that it takes to fight your way back from an assault that huge. Exceptional qualities like determination, discipline, persistence, optimism, audacity and plain, bloody stubbornness. And I knew Glenn had all these qualities in spades. And above all else, you also need a massive work ethic—and I knew Glenn possessed a work ethic like no one else I've ever met—well, maybe except for Jono!

'Destiny' … funny old word, that. The Oxford Dictionary defines this word as: 'predetermined events'. Some people believe that our destiny is mapped out for us when we're born. Others believe that we are responsible for determining or creating our own destiny. You've heard the sayings, 'everything happens for a reason', or 'we make our own luck'. Well, sometimes bad things happen to good people for no damn reason.

Few of us go through life unscathed by tragedy of some kind, so at times it may be very hard to accept that 'everything happens for a reason'. And honestly, I really loathe that line! Because sometimes we don't get a choice in our destiny. It's taken out of our hands. And all we can do is either take what has been dealt and either allow it to make us better people—bigger people—or allow it to tear us down. That choice does not belong to destiny; that choice belongs to us.

Sadly, you will never truly understand who you are, and how strong you are, until you develop real courage by surviving challenges like Glenn and his family. And courage doesn't mean you don't feel fear. Sometimes being afraid allows you to find your courage. But let me finish on a positive note. I've travelled the world talking to clinicians about never giving up on recovery from brain injury. In Melbourne a recent study proved that recovery can take place ten-plus years out from an incident. In the years since Jono's accident, I can honestly say he continues to improve because he continues to put in.

So, my friends, there is no expiry date on Glenn's recovery. It's still early days, and the future holds so much promise. There's no two-year plateau that doctors and clinicians would have you believe because it saves thousands of dollars from their precious medical funding to cut you off from rehab.

Yes, you need exceptional motivation and self-drive; an intense, frequent and prolonged rehabilitation programme; plus, the love and support of family and caring friends.

Fortunately, GW, you have all that in spades too!

Your job now is to write your own ending to this gutsy story (and when you're done, I'll write your book).

Finally, Glenn, as you continue on your way onwards and upwards, never ever let someone else's doubts blur your own vision.

* * *

Book promotions, signings, and guest-speaking opportunities continued to flood in—the latter mostly through word of mouth. Fortunately, I now had Rob to drive me around Sydney; for some time he had only been working weekends so that he could care for me and help me care for Jon.

Six months after the book's release something quite extraordinary occurred, something that demonstrates the magic of books and the far-reaching capacity of the written word ... of how words can open doors and hearts, and connect us with others.

On a sleepy Monday morning in January 2016, I had a phone call from Ohio in the USA, from a man who said he was tracing his family tree. At first, I thought it was a prank call (it was early, I was drowsy!) but as he talked, words and names began to register and take shape in my mind. He said he had been tracing my grandmother, Annus (Anna) Loew, who came to Australia after the war, six years after her two sons, Frici and Gyuri (Fred and George). And importantly, he revealed details that were not included in *With Just One Suitcase*—other family names, places, events, and so forth. His search had brought him to a frustrating full stop some years ago until someone from the Australian Jewish Genealogical Society (whom he had been liaising with during his protracted search) let him know she had read an article in *The Age* newspaper about a man called Frederic Loew and his daughter who had written his life story in a book called *With Just One Suitcase*. He immediately bought a copy of the book online and in his words, devoured it.

Within a few short days of finishing it, Vladimir Roth tracked me down via the internet and called me. He turned out to be my father's second cousin. When I relayed our conversation to Dad—who had always believed that *all* his relatives had tragically died in the Holocaust—he was overcome with emotion. Vladimir informed me of other living distant members of our clan spread throughout England and Europe who had reconnected and had been meeting for family reunions every few years.

Since then, we have kept in contact via email and when Dad last visited from Melbourne, we Skyped each other, speaking for over an hour. Many times throughout this emotional conversation, Dad wiped away tears as he said, 'Vlado, I feel like I'm looking at myself—only 20 years younger!'

Some months afterwards, another significant phone call occurred which again demonstrates the power of the written word. This time it was from a retired neurologist who had recently read my book. My mother-in-law, Stephanie, was astonished to hear the voice of her daughter's specialist after a lapse of some 30 years. Rosemary was only 50 when her battle with the rare and crippling neurological disease metachromatic leukodystrophy (MLD)[2] ended in 2002.

In Chapter 12 of the book, I had described the pain and devastation Rob's parents suffered when given a terminal prognosis for their already incapacitated daughter. During that call to Stephanie, Dr Pryor informed her that although unnamed, he realised he was actually reading about himself in Chapter 12 of my book! He went on to say how much he learnt from reading first-hand what parents like my in-laws faced when dealt such a heavy hand from providence. Of course, he held enormous compassion for all his patients and their families, but I believe he hadn't truly placed himself in their shoes until that moment. Reading this section of the book gave him great insight, he said. The capacity of stories to evoke empathy.

However, what wasn't mentioned in that chapter, because it was some years later and when I was six months pregnant with Jon, I was informed that MLD is a genetic disorder. We immediately made an appointment to see Dr Pryor, who referred me to a geneticist at Sydney University. I can't recall his name, but I do remember sitting anxiously at a desk in

---

2. Metachromatic leukodystrophy, the most common form of leukodystrophy, is a rare inherited neurometabolic disorder affecting the white matter of the brain (leukoencephalopathy). It is characterised by the accumulation of a fatty substance known as sulphatide (a sphingolipid) in the brain and other areas of the body (i.e., liver, gall bladder, kidneys, and/or spleen). The fatty protective covering on the nerve fibres (myelin) is lost from areas of the central nervous system (CNS) due to the buildup of sulfatide. Symptoms of metachromatic leukodystrophy may include convulsions, seizures, personality changes, spasticity, progressive dementia, motor disturbances progressing to paralysis, and/or visual impairment leading to blindness. https://rarediseases.org/rare-diseases/metachromatic-leukodystrophy/

his empty lecture room with Rob holding my hand, just as anxious as me, whilst the geneticist scribbled out flow charts filled with statistics on his blackboard. Basically, he confirmed my worst fear: MLD is caused by defective genes. However, he went on to explain that not everyone who inherits a defective gene will develop it. Being a recessive gene, for a person to develop the disease, these genes must be inherited from both parents. If a child inherits only one defective gene, he or she is a carrier of the disease, but is unlikely to develop MLD.

We left our lesson on the workings of genetics behind us that day in 1984. But the knowledgeable geneticist's final words will stay with me always: 'Your husband has a 66 percent chance of being a carrier of MLD. But go away and forget about it. Really. You have more chance of your child being hit by a car.'

*　*　*

In April 2016, I was given the amazing opportunity of being invited to give an address to students graduating from Macquarie University. The topic was: 'You can change the world', to be addressed in ten minutes, no less! After careful consideration I knew exactly what I wanted to say to young people about to embark on life after university. Changing the world is a great aspiration, but the reality is that few individuals become global leaders. My message was going to be that if you get the chance to touch the life of even *one* person, not only are you changing their world, but you're giving yourself a much bigger gift than you're giving them.

The day arrived and I wasn't in the least bit nervous. Being well prepared, having time to rehearse, and being passionate about your underlying message, I find, contribute to self-confidence. (To think I wouldn't even put my hand up to answer a question at school, to now having the confidence to speak in front of thousands!).

Following a hearty address from a relaxed, informal Chancellor, my turn to step up to the podium arrived. In returning to his seat, as we passed, the Chancellor leant in and whispered: 'Take your time, you can go over ten minutes, no problem'.

With that, I relaxed even more, and ad-libbed and joked asides with the carefree Chancellor. Fortunately, the audience laughed in all the right places.

Macquarie University Keynote Graduation Speech
12 April 2016
'You Can Change the World'

I would like to begin by acknowledging the traditional custodians of this land, the Daruk people, and pay my respects to elders, both past and present.

Chancellor, Vice Chancellor, members of faculty, staff, distinguished guests, graduates and proud family and friends.

I am very honoured to be invited to speak here today at Macquarie University—one of Australia's finest. My sincere congratulations to each of the graduates on this significant milestone. I have a son who is a structural engineer so I understand just how hard you have all worked: the all-nighters fuelled with coffee, energy drinks and junk food; the unkempt appearance; the vagabond stench—or was it just my son who, for much of his uni life, resembled Tom Hanks from *Castaway*!

Despite the kind introduction by the Chancellor, right now most of you are probably wondering 'who the heck is this strange lady—

what makes her so special?' Well, let me state up front that there is nothing particularly special about me. First and foremost, I am just your average wife and mum, and like a lot of people here today, I wear many hats. My most important job, however, and the one I identify with best, is that of being a carer.

Identity is important. Identity makes us unique. Not only is it how we view ourselves, but also how the world views us. However, in Australian culture, identity is tied closely to profession. Often, after introductions are made, the first question we are asked is: 'What do you do?' And, of course, if the response is to the effect of: 'I work in medicine, law, government, or perhaps even Chancellor of the university', most of us would have a similar reaction of: 'hmm, quite impressive'. But what if the answer came back as: 'My name is Cheryl Koenig and I am a carer'. What would you think of me ... really?

Like it or not, there's a sense of esteem that is attached to occupation. But regardless of societal status, culture or creed, caring is an integral part of life. Because the reality is, no matter what letters or titles you have before or after your name, there are only four categories of people in this world: those who have been carers; those who are currently carers; those who will be carers; and those who will need carers.

So, let me introduce myself again, and perhaps give you a better sense of the esteem I attach to caring. Here I go. 'Hello, my name is Cheryl Koenig. What is it I do, you ask? Why, I have THE single most important job in the world—I am a carer! What's that? You heard I was an author of four books, Australia Day Ambassador, New South Wales Woman of the Year, and the recipient of an OAM for my charity work? Oh well, yes, that's all good and true, and don't get me wrong, it's terribly important work...

But above all that—in fact, towering way above—is my role as the carer of my adorable 31-year-old son who was hit by a speeding car when aged just 12 and sustained an extremely severe traumatic brain injury.

It's the job I am most proud of. It tells you more about me, my values and ethos, than any other role or accolade. And in my opinion, there is no job more worthwhile than enhancing the health and happiness of someone that you love, because in that very act, you are changing their world for the better.

As individuals inspired by your teachings from within these hallowed halls, your values and ambitions may lie in tackling vital issues like environmental sustainability, cultural conservation, or social justice. Never underestimate that your actions, however small, or in any arena, have the power to add up to great changes to the world of your choosing.

Having a desire to impart 'global change' is admirable, but global change is the work or governance by many people at various levels. I believe the true marker of success is measured not by the scale of change, but rather by constructive change to even one person's world.

Leadership and change can happen in your home, your community, your workplace. It will happen wherever you're passionate about your cause and determined to work hard.

Without doubt your degrees would have taught you that having a positive mindset helps tackle life's challenges (such as the stress of exam times … I bet you're glad they're over!). But it's also true in broader terms. A positive thinker will see the opportunity within any difficulty, whilst a negative thinker sees only the difficulty.

Today, of course, is a happy occasion. But it is a profound truth that few of us go through life without personal adversity. I believe we learn more from sadness or difficulty, than from any other time. So, I'll give you an example of my family's journey, as I also believe that it is a human need to be told stories—about who we are, why we are, where we've come from—so we know what may be possible.

Things were going perfectly well for my little family up until our son, Jonathan, got hit by a car. Then, not just his, but all our lives got turned upside down. We were told by the experts that if he survived, he would probably never walk, talk or eat again. Well, we weren't going to settle for that, were we? (and here I recall ad-libbing). 'Stubborn' you say … my bloody oath!' (I then turned to the Chancellor behind me and said jokingly, 'Is that okay, Chancellor? Can I say that?' To which he replied 'Yes, yes, my word, yes!').

No one was going to tell me what my son's potential was going to be. I wasn't going to let the negative thinkers shape his destiny, nor his identity. So Team Jono set to work, and for the next decade my husband and I worked eight to ten hours a day on his physical and cognitive rehabilitation—and today he not only walks well, but can run, swim laps, play tennis, ski, drive and he works five days a week in four different jobs.

Now that's determination; his determination. And that's courage. And courage doesn't mean you don't experience fear. Courage means you don't let the fear stop you!

I believe the most crucial investment we can as make as individuals is in our shared social well-being. Generosity—giving back to society— is an expression of spirit, and spirit is priceless. Your spirit, as you are now passed the baton of humanity, will cultivate the fundamental principles required to allow those marginalised (like carers, the displaced, the homeless) to become members of modern society with human rights such as equality and autonomy. And, of course, what I alluded to earlier: respect and dignity.

Finally, as you write the next chapter of your lives, my wish is that you identify with the group of positive thinkers. No matter what life challenges you face, find the opportunity within the difficulty. Don't be afraid to take risks, to stumble and fall. Because only through hitting the ground, can you experience the feeling of triumph that comes from the climb back up, and go forward to make the world—your world—a better place.

After my speech I was, naturally, thanked and told I did well by the Chancellor, attending faculty and staff. However, as we were about to leave the auditorium, the Vice Chancellor quickly approached Rob and me. He told us that he had taught all around the world and attended many, many graduations and heard many inspiring speeches, but that mine, was the best and most moving he had ever heard.

'Thank you, so much, but I'm sure you've heard better,' I replied, humbled by his remarks.

'Believe me … I'm not saying it because I *have* to. I am saying it because it's true.'

It took about an hour for us to leave the garden reception as there was a line-up of students and parents waiting to talk to me.

One kind lady said: 'That was the most inspirational speech I have ever heard. I have bought the video so I can replay your words over and over.'

But the most important feedback came from Chris, who downloaded the speech on YouTube the next day. I could tell he wasn't overly impressed with my gag about him resembling Tom Hanks from *Castaway*, but he laughed about it regardless. However, he told me that what inspired him most and what he would try to use in his own life, was my reflections on about courage: that it was okay to feel afraid but that you shouldn't let the fear stop you.

* * *

Ironically, I was forced to translate my own words into action when, in late 2016, after seven years of remission, severe nausea and constant diarrhoea saw my weight plummet to that of my chemotherapy days. Along with increased levels of pain, I was sickly and emaciated. By mid-afternoon most days, I had trouble standing. If I made plans, even coffee with friends, it had to be in the morning. But if I had diarrhoea, naturally everything had to be cancelled. The neuropathic pain became so extreme at night, I dreaded going to bed. It seemed to lie in ambush, just waiting for me to close my eyes. The intensity of the pain (which unfortunately continues to this day) varied from that of a razor-sharp knife being slid down the outside of both legs, to a deep-seated bone-crushing pain in both my arms and legs as if they were being crushed in a vice, to electric shock-like spasms. Heat exacerbates the pain and sometimes the only relief I can get on a hot night is standing thigh-deep in our swimming pool until my legs are chilled.

Everyone was worried. I was already under the care of two specialists—Professor Peter Youssef, a highly respected rheumatologist of gentle disposition and comforting manner, who was doing an excellent job at managing my Sjogren's disease. And Professor Michael Barnett, an energetic neurologist with a sharp intellect and quick turn of mind diagnostically, whom I saw every six months for routine check-ups regarding my transverse myelitis. However, because of the extreme weight loss, they both suggested I make an appointment with my cancer specialist, haematologist Professor John Gibson.

Being back in the haematology clinic at the RPA with those pour souls who were on the path I had once trodden, was deeply unsettling. So, too, was Professor Gibson's serious disposition at seeing me; nothing like the good-natured, jovial man I recalled. As he listened to my symptoms his face was grave.

'Cheryl,' he said, 'it's time for another PET scan'.

'Okay.' I knew he'd suggest that.

'I'll organise it immediately.'

Within a few days Rob, Jon and I made our way back to the RPA for a full-body nuclear scan. We didn't need to be told what they were looking for. Naturally, Rob was worried, as was Jon; and Chris too, whose text messages revealed his quiet fear.

'Don't worry,' I assured all of them. 'I'm positive all will be fine.'

One week later on our return visit to Professor Gibson for the results of the scan, this time he was smiling as we walked into his small office, just like the kindly man I remembered.

'All clear,' he said with obvious relief. He went on to suggest that my medications be reduced as I was so underweight that the high doses needed to keep the Sjogren's and other neuropathic pain at bay were most likely compounding any digestion issues associated with my type of auto-immune disease. He also suggested I see a dietician to help me gain weight.

Following his advice, things have improved but it's not all plain sailing. I am now lactose intolerant so have eliminated most dairy products from my diet and, on the advice of the dietician, adopted a very high fibre diet which has reduced my gut-related problems. This has significantly improved my daily life as I'm not tied to the bathroom for five days out of every seven. I know I'm still underweight—people have no hesitation in passing comment on my skeletal appearance—but I am eating well (most days) and I do feel better in that department than I have for a very long time.

Despite my vexing aches and pains, I am trying hard not to be one.

17

Minted gratitude

November 2016

Broadbeach, Queensland: my family's favourite beach. We had travelled to this beautiful part of Australia to celebrate the amazing accomplishment of Steven and Stephanie's 65th wedding anniversary. Not many have the good fortune to reach such a milestone, but then again, not many show the devotion, commitment and respect to one another as do my in-laws. To be part of their dance through the symphony of life with all its high and low notes has been a privilege. Stephanie has always said, 'Growing old with your partner is better than winning the lottery'.

As I relaxed on the beach in the mildness of a glorious spring day and watched the sun flicker across the teal-blue ocean, glistening like diamonds upon the crest of each ripple, with the smell of the sea salt and other sweet beach aromas tickling my senses, it wasn't hard to be happy, to feel alive, content and grateful again.

Gratitude is often misunderstood, seen as a payment or due, when in fact it is a gift. The feeling of gratitude should not be objectified. In my experience it is a trait common to those who live serenely; and I am very cognisant of the gift of a unique set of circumstances that conspired in my survival with a brush against cancer. Importantly, I understand my survival was also determined by the vagaries of my particular type and stage of cancer, not by any personal willpower or inner strength. Sure, these days life is still testing me, and it takes some of those qualities to get up and get on with it, but I am grateful for the opportunity to embrace each sunrise.

This particular morning, however, observing my family interact lovingly in the spray of the cool waters, ever so gently, from behind darkened sunglasses tears escaped of their own volition. For I was finally where my mind took me to escape all those long, lonely nights in the cold hard hospital bed where I'd missed the warmth of Rob's silhouette. It is the place to where I'd retreated following each chemotherapy treatment as I lay in my own bed, immobile with nausea and fatigue. And the place where I had 'virtually' escaped during the perfunctory intimidation of radiotherapy burning my skin.

I want for nothing more than what I have this day: Rob holding my hand, his love constant, tender and giving; the one I hold when there's nothing to hold onto. Some people have stratospheric expectations of what love looks like. I don't have to look to the stratosphere … I only have to look down to the hand still holding mine.

Chris, my fine flawless one, who has become even more perfect as he fills the frame of doting husband and father; so happy with the love of his life, Danielle who has added a new dimension, a sweetness to our lives. And together they have produced the blessing that is Summer Rachel Koenig who was eleven months old (now, in 2019, three years old, since joined by 19-month-old sister, Oliva Jasmine Koenig).

Being a grandmother is precious beyond words. More so, as for the first time since my life-threatening illness, I can hear my mortality whispering in my ear. I know with certainty that my granddaughters will grow up and I will die—that's the cycle of life. But right now, the unknown brevity of our relationship only adds to its passion.

At a time in my life where I thought I had already lived my best day, reached my tallest high, I wasn't expecting the depth of euphoria that being a grandmother brings, that my adoration would hit me afresh like a heavenly breeze. Ripeness is all, says the poet, and holding a child of my child in my arms gives me no greater sense of completeness, of coming full circle. The shelves of books with my name on them, the medals and awards, pale into insignificance. My greatest accomplishment is becoming a grandmother—an achievement which, of course, took no effort from me.

However, on this celebratory family holiday, observing little Summer smile, laugh, and discover the world, is gratifying beyond words. Of course, she is a beautiful cherub—no bias there! More importantly, she is a cheerful little girl who carries a quietly determined spirit. And to Nanny K's great delight, adores books and reading time.

There is so much to be grateful for in the preservation and perseverance of my precious rose: Jonathan Steven Koenig. No more fitting namesake for him to carry than that of his paternal grandfather, Steven. For with that comes a DNA of steely resolve and boundless courage. Jon, with his ever-curious mind and affable nature, still needing my presence, my nurturing. His countless achievements fill me with pride, as does his ability to touch and inspire. And while ever this body of mine contains the slightest of breath, caring for Jon's needs will continue to be my priority and my privilege. However, it would be duplicitous of me to not to admit that even after 20 years, there are still moments where I grieve for the son I have *not* lost. Exceptional as Jon is, still I grieve. Not for myself, but rather for him and the experiences he will never have. A part of him will never be, and I feel the loss and pain of that.

Nonetheless, on this perfect day at the beach I enjoyed the serenity as I basked in the radiance of my special family. For like the early morning surfers paddling for that perfect wave, the joggers and walkers pounding the boardwalk for that perfect body, I realised that I, too, had worked hard for my life, with its successes and shortcomings. And I knew that I would never, ever, let go of it without a fight, now or in the future, as it is a life worth fighting for. All life is.

18

We travel not to escape life, but for life not to escape us

As the seasons swept by, my daily life continued to be fluid—a fine balancing act of caring for my family, as well as worrying about and assisting where possible with age-related issues concerning Steven and Stephanie, and my father Fred. With my health issues and my weight, again, plummeting, my advocacy work on behalf of other carers and people with disability continued, yet regrettably in a much-reduced capacity. Sometimes it was difficult to look for possibilities; truth be told, there were many days when the surrounding negativity of illness weighed heavily, blurring my usual rose-coloured glasses.

For over a decade, Rob had steadfastly refused to take me out of the country, due to my medical status. And as much as I nagged him—especially every time an advertisement came on the television for alluring European river cruises from Amsterdam to Budapest—in all honesty, who could blame him? Ironically it was yet another serious medical hiccup one day in April 2017 which saw him change his stance.

One night I went to bed with a massive headache. The next morning when I got out of bed, I felt a little off-balance, so was stumbling around using the walls for support, thinking it was another episode of vertigo. However, I soon realised

I couldn't hear properly with my right ear. 'I must have water in it,' I said to Rob, as I went about the day clutching onto anything stable and hopping on one leg with my head tilted. Despite my efforts to clear a feeling of cottonwool wedged in my ear, it persisted.

Autumn and its cooler nights should have brought me some relief from my weird but not wonderful neuropathic leg pain. Now, even lightweight cotton sheets touching my legs felt like sheets of iron. And whilst I lay there in the darkness trying to meditate, focus on my breathing and tell myself I was fine, I realised that I had a ringing sound in one or perhaps both ears. It sounded as if we had left the windows open on a sultry summer night and the distinctive high-pitched song of cicadas had invaded our bedroom.

It took me two weeks to get myself to the doctor who prescribed a cortisone spray in case I had blocked sinus, which did nothing to help. Finally, some weeks later, I went to see an ear, nose and throat specialist who ordered audio testing and an MRI of my brain. He believed I had suffered a mini bleed on my brain (TIA[1]) most likely from one of the many small white-matter hyperintensities that now littered my brain like a person in their 80s, rather than their 50s

---

1. A transient ischaemic attack (TIA) is a minor stroke and provides a powerful warning that a stroke may occur in the following hours, days, weeks or months. It happens when blood going to the brain is stopped and then starts again. Blood is carried to the brain by blood vessels and a blood clot may cause a blockage that prevents blood moving through an artery. In some cases, a TIA may be caused by a small bleed in the brain. For more information on signs, symptoms and treatment, visit: https://www.betterhealth.vic.gov.au/health/conditionsandtreatments/transient-ischaemic-attack-tia

(actual cause of these small white lesions could either be from the transverse myelitis, or even Sjogren's disease which causes damage to all organs of the body).

The ENT specialist said any sudden sensorineural hearing loss (SSHL[2]) should be treated as an emergency and I should have gone straight to my local hospital's emergency department, as sometimes if treated promptly it can be rectified with steroid treatment. However, six or more weeks down the track, the specialist believed my bleed had permanently damaged a nerve that leads to the ear, and therefore, steroids would now be useless.

'Great,' I said to Rob after the diagnosis. 'Another thing to add to the ever-growing list.'

But it was the ominous predictions by the ENT specialist which—forgive the pun—kept ringing in my ears for days. He said that having had one TIA, I now fell into a high-risk demographic for recurrence of TIAs, and it also increased my chance of having a larger stroke by a staggering 150% more than the average.

'Rob,' I said over breakfast one brisk autumn morning, the sternness of my tone taking him by surprise, 'I feel like a ticking time bomb. I don't want to sit around waiting for

---

2. Sudden sensorineural hearing loss (SSHL) is also known as sudden deafness. It occurs when you lose your hearing very quickly, typically only in one ear. It can happen instantly or over several days. During this time, sound gradually becomes muffled or faint. SSHL happens when the inner ear, the cochlea in the inner ear, or the nerve pathways between the ear and the brain become damaged. Some possible causes include: head injury; prolonged exposure to loud noise; neurologic conditions, immune system disease; ageing and others which can be found at: http://www.healthline.com/health/sensorineural-deafness#causes2.

something to happen. I don't want life to pass us by from the perimeters. I am sick of being sick. Sick of being weak. And sick of everyone treating me like I'm sick and weak!'

'But you don't sit around, Chez. You never stop. And we don't treat you like that, do we?'

'Oh, you all might think you don't, but believe me you do. Not that I don't appreciate everyone's concern. It's just I don't want to feel *dependent* anymore. Frankly, I don't want to be *that* person. I need to do something. Life's been too stressful of late. I need to find happiness in other things, in other places … not rely on others to make me *feel* happy … to make me feel capable. You know what I mean?'

He did. Of course, he did. He knew what was inside my heart and mind even before it reached my lips. He understood. At times, I felt not just unwanted, but even worse, ignored or forgotten. This, of course, speaks to the broader human need: we all need to be needed. Being needed consists of a natural human hunger to help others. Feeling redundant is a blow to the human spirit.

Following my outpouring to Rob, thoughts which had hung heavy since the specialist's portentous prognosis now became as clear as a shallow stream. As I sipped my lemon tea in the briskness of that autumn morning, I took a long stroll through the hall of mirrors and realised the time had come to regain control of my life; to reject weakness and withdrawal. To defiantly be that glass-half-full person again. To rediscover that little bit of 'me' I had let slip away.

'We're going to do that European river cruise, okay, Rob?' It was more of a statement than a question.

'Chez, honey,' he replied with his usual exasperation at the mention of such an arduous adventure. 'We've discussed it before. I, and the doctors, don't think you can make the long-haul trip to Europe. Let alone overtax yourself and risk a hospital admission overseas. Think about it.' Then, recognising a long-absent look of determination etched upon my face, he added: 'Okay, even if we did go, we'd need to do more while we were there—not just spend two weeks on a boat.'

That was all the encouragement I needed. 'I can make it, Rob, and we will do more. I'll get myself stronger first, I promise.'

I kept my promise and stepped up my meagre exercise program straightaway. The problem I have had with any form of exercise is that after just a few minutes it triggers tremors and vibrations in my legs, and once I've crossed that line, I know I'm heading for more pain. But, as the saying goes: what doesn't kill you…

* * *

Three months later, after a tiring fifteen-hour flight—mostly spent regretting that welcome champagne as I repeatedly staggered to the bathroom with stomach cramps (avoiding eye contact with Rob on my way)—the 42-degree heat of Dubai hit me like a sledgehammer. On arrival at our Jumeirah beach hotel, I must have looked as bedraggled as I felt because the receptionist kindly upgraded our room to an apartment, with uninterrupted views of Dubai's looming high-rise city and harbour from every window.

Over our two-night stopover we ventured out twice from the welcome oasis of air conditioning. On our first expedition we were tempted by glimpses of the nearby beach, however, the water temperature was like that of a hot spa, providing no relief from the searing heat. Our second outing was, therefore, more sensibly to the world's largest shopping complex, the Dubai Mall, where we marvelled at the extravagant gold features and gazed with wonder at the indoor winter wonderland of a snow-covered ski-field.

A further seven-hour flight took us to Venice. From the moment our water taxi spirited us between the colourful buildings hugging the foreshore of the Grand Canal, I knew the place I had spent a lifetime dreaming about was going to be unforgettable. For five nights we lived like Venetians in a quirky little apartment with exposed slanted wooden beams that we needed to duck our heads to walk beneath, and which Rob christened 'the Endeavour' after James Cook's ship. It had a small rooftop balcony on which we could quench our thirst after a long day exploring colourful canals and quaint alleyways. Even though I had increased my level of fitness as best I could before the trip, the first few days capturing all Venice had to offer caused extreme pain and exhaustion. But did I complain? Not on your nelly! Here I was in one of the world's most stunningly unique cities. Here I was in *Venice*. Yes, I know … it was hard for even me to believe.

The rhythm of Venice enveloped us in its eccentric ensemble of culture, architecture, vibrant people and matchless beauty. Each day we flocked, with a pandemonium of tourists who posed under classic facades. We were enamoured by the passion of gossiping locals and shopkeepers who beckoned from under canopies of endless cafés and gelato shops. And we were mesmerised by the sight and sound of a serpentine line of gondolas—the staccato pitch of flirtatious gondoliers, their oars caressing the water, filtered up as we crossed over decorative stone bridges. Like 20 million tourists each year, we, too, would have our ride along the pulsing veins of Venice.

After several days of this fantastical ensemble, I discovered it was also the little things about Venice that added to its charm. Our final evening was spent, drink in hand, on our rooftop balcony. As we looked out over terracotta roofs, the sound of a nearby church choir drifted up, their heavenly harmonies bidding us farewell. As I held Rob's hand and peered at the street lamps, I noticed the beauty of their subtle shade of amethyst. Sadly resigned, I whispered goodbye to the 'city of love' which had lived up to its name and so much more. *Venezia, la bella città, ti amerò per sempre*[3].

After a two-hour fast train trip, we arrived in Florence where we spent five days exploring this city of renaissance and romanticism, and the ridiculously beautiful landscapes of surrounding Tuscany: Pisa, Sienna, Cinque Terre—the last filled with colourful buildings dotting the plunging coastline. Florence was more than the sum of its glorious Renaissance past, world-class art and endearing stereotypes. Beneath the terracotta domes of some of the most awe-inspiring churches and museums I had ever seen, I found Florence to be dynamic and chic. A place to find pleasure in the unity and connection to humanity that a strong culture brings. As I looked up to take in the stunning frescos, golden cornices and arches laced

---

3. Venice, beautiful city, I will always love you.

with intricate history, I was spiritually moved by this myriad of delights, and I was reminded of the necessity to always *look up*.

Our next stop was Amsterdam—the city of bikes, canals and pot-aroma cafes on every corner. We had two days there before we embarked on a 15-day journey down the Rhine, Main and Danube Rivers to Budapest. We almost missed our ship's departure, though, as I was too ill with severe tummy troubles to leave the sanctuary of the hotel bathroom. Somehow, I pulled it together just in time for a quick taxi ride to port.

On board our luxurious ship, *MS Amavenita*, our days were filled with first-class comfort, degustation of the limitless, indulgent food (usually reflecting whatever region we were sailing through), discovery of fine friendships, along with intimate views of picture-postcard European cities and towns.

After an embarkation process of a welcome champagne to meet the captain and crew (of which there were 50 to service the 150 passengers), we were divided into four different groups based on mobility and preferred choice of sightseeing for each day's activity. Naively, after so much walking in Venice and Florence, I had imagined I would be able to rest up on board the cruise. Far from it! Each day, as soon as the sun peeked its way over a semi-foggy Father Rhine, the action began, and very often didn't end until late at night after a splendid dinner and entertainment, either on board themed to suit the region in which we were sailing, or an on-shore excursion where we enjoyed classical concerts performed in magical castles.

At first, Jon and I elected to venture out each day at a slow pace along with the ten or so other passengers whose ambulation troubled them. However, by the second week, we found ourselves progressing up through the divided groups of ability; we were determined to explore as much of the sights and atmosphere as we possibly could.

From our first stop in Cologne, with its awe-inspiring cathedral, *Kölner Dom* (whose construction began in 1248 and took 600 years to complete), along the 1,820 kilometres of arguably Europe's most scenic river system (via the man-made Rhine-Maine-Danube Canals which took some 30 years to construct, consisting of 68 river locks which lower and raise ships as necessary), until we docked opposite the majestic Houses of Parliament in cosmopolitan Budapest in Hungary, the marvellous mediaeval architecture in towns such as Rothenberg, Miltenberg, Würzburg, Bamberg and others, made me realise that we were standing where much of our civilised world began. The religion, politics, architecture and literature of early civilisations like the Romans, Ottomans, Barbarians, etcetera, from this part of Europe, have perhaps unknowingly melded and shaped much of our life today. However, being surrounded now by these cultures—frozen like music, in time—cultivated my quest for enlightenment of our roots for the entirety of the trip.

Along the way, it had come to the attention of the cruise director (who must have googled me) that I was an author and motivational speaker. She asked if I would like to speak to the passengers about my books and my family's history—naturally, including Jon's story, about which so many people had already asked. I agreed to speak as both Rob and I were keenly aware of everybody's natural curiosity and sensed a genuine sympathy towards our little threesome.

This was especially evident one evening when the ship's after-dinner entertainment included waltzing to the sound of a melodious pianist. As Jon and I fumbled our way around the small dance floor, a delicately framed Irish lady with tears freely flowing down her cheeks approached me and took Jon's embrace from me to her, at the same time telling me that I should be dancing with my husband. Others around began to cry. Sure, I get it, people feel for us, but they needn't—and that's what my speech that week would focus on: please don't feel sorry for us … Yes, we've been to hell and back, but we're in a happy place now. I was also able to tell everyone on board all about Jon's remarkable achievements.

After that talk the current shifted, and those who were apprehensive about approaching Jon and initiating conversation, changed tack. Suddenly he was front and centre at every event, with fellow passengers all wanting a piece of him! Hearing him engage in conversation in his usual witty manner, was a joy.

To one person I heard him say: 'Having a brain injury is a lot like a football match. You have to suffer the blows, get back up and get on with the game.' To another, who asked him if he had any memory problems, he replied: 'No. My brain is like a camera. Only problem is sometimes I forget to put the sim card in!' And when asked what he liked about his jobs, he replied: 'I love my work because they all accept me, and it makes me feel like a useful person.'

As the cruise drifted onward, Jon became—as one passenger so kindly put it—'the life and soul of the ship'. We were told by others that just watching him pack in as much as he could despite the arduousness of the organised schedule, inspired them to do the same.

Yes, Jon has that effect on people. I've often said to him that despite his assortment of clerical and factory jobs, his *main* job, each and every day as he leaves home to go to work or elsewhere, is that of a *teacher*. A teacher of tolerance, compassion, understanding, and most importantly, patience and persistence. In a world filled with apathy in lieu of empathy, and satisfaction revolving around instant gratification, his ability to press on regardless of a body that won't always comply like that of his peers, his ability to teach others the true order of the importance of things, is his gift.

Amongst all the beautiful cities we visited, Vienna was indeed a highlight. On every street corner, behind the ornamental façades of Parliament House, City Hall (*Rathaus*), the Opera House, St Stephen's Cathedral and all along the *Ringstrasse* (a road which encircles the city centre), majestic palaces, elegant residences and museums, lavishly decorated and filled with incredible royal history, abounded.

'Vienna, or *Wien* as your Uncle Nick was so fond of saying, is just so elegant. The grandest of cities I've seen so far,' I enthused, as we enjoyed an authentic Wiener Schnitzel in a café in the *Naschmarkt* (a local street market filled with cafés, and fruit and vegetable stalls). 'I need more than just a day here. One day we will simply have to come back.'

The ship did offer a second day of sightseeing in Vienna, but also on offer was a day trip to Bratislava. We chose option two as I'd learnt during the unexpected phone call from my father's second cousin, Vladimir, that I had a relative living there. So, through Vladamir (and Tom Seiden, a dear Roth cousin in England who has created a fantastic online family heritage site) I organised a visit to meet Viera, my second cousin, once removed.

Bratislava ('Brat' meaning brother, 'Slava' meaning glory) is Slovakia's capital. Slovakia became independent from Czechoslovakia in the early 1990s and has recently enjoyed a renaissance in culture and rebuilding.

I saw Viera standing in the centre of the Old Town Square just as we had earlier planned. Rob, Jon and I had just finished our pre-arranged city tour and were organising a place to re-join our group for the bus trip back to port.

I slowly walked up to Viera, admiring her confident posture and well-kept appearance. 'Viera?' I inquired, even though I knew her reply. 'Hi … I'm Cheryl.' She embraced me, kissing me on both cheeks. Fortunately, her English was excellent and after introducing Rob and Jon, she showed us around the city square and eventually took us down a small dark alley which led to a dimly lit restaurant—one which we would never have thought to try out for ourselves. The food, which we found heavily influenced by its Hungarian neighbour, was excellent. We spent almost two hours together chatting about our lives, catching up on who lived where and how exactly we were linked, before suddenly, it was time to go.

On the walk back through the town centre, I stopped to look at a souvenir shop that was displaying Christmas decorations which I was collecting from each city we visited. Viera insisted on paying for a large Christmas tree bauble with *Bratislava* written across it. I relented, only because as I told her, each Christmas when I hang the delicate bauble on my tree, I will think of her and our special time together in Bratislava.

As we sailed down the blue carpet of the Danube into the Hungarian capital and our fabulous trip on board the *Amavenita* drew to its conclusion, despite never having been to Budapest before, I was overwhelmed by a feeling of familiarity. Docked for our last night on board, we were treated to a wonderful meal of Hungarian goulash with traditional trimmings and luscious creamy tortes for dessert. Gazing out the ship's dining-room window, we were welcomed to our ancestral roots by a splendorous moon shining brightly over the Houses of Parliament.

This was not quite the end of our trip of a lifetime. If anything, it was more like the beginning. After an early morning disembarkation, we were bussed to Budapest Airport from where most of our fellow passengers flew home. However, we had pre-arranged to meet up with Evelyn, Rob's first cousin of Romanian heritage, slightly younger in vintage than he, whose confident gregarious personality was infectious.

Evelyn had jumped at the opportunity to fly in from her home town in Germany and join us on our three-day pilgrimage driving across the border to Timişoara. She was born in Timişoara but had left some 20 years ago with her daughter, Patricia, to begin a new life for herself and her parents. Her mother, Hermina, was Rob's Dad's sister, but had passed away some years ago, followed shortly thereafter by her father, Ludwig.

It had been nearly 20 years since we had all been together, when she visited Australia shortly after Jon's accident, so it was an emotional reunion. Evelyn took control of the hire car and the situation, as she was fluent in Hungarian and Romanian as well as English and German. She was an excellent guide and fantastic company over the next three days.

The drive from Budapest to Timişoara should have taken three hours with Evelyn doing speeds of up to 200 kilometres per hour, except for two things: firstly the border patrol crossing from Hungary into Romania took around half an hour in a queue of cars stretching back many kilometres, and secondly, because we were so busy catching up on each other's lives, we missed the Timişoara turn-off so had to drive another 15 minutes along the highway before we could safely do a U-turn.

The drive itself was filled with evidence of a rich and fertile land (just as I had included in the first chapter of *With Just One Suitcase*, using our dads' memories and my imagination) with rolling plains of sunflowers, tall and reaching skyward, stretching as far as the eye could see (forget Tuscany, I say!).

On arrival at the outskirts of the city of both our fathers' birth, now inhabited by a population of around 300,000, the tall grey, almost lifeless buildings were reminiscent of a bygone utilitarian era—communism—with stark reminders of a poor and forgotten people.

In the city centre, our pre-booked Hotel Savoy was easily located, and we were shown to our fourth-floor room, through the atrium foyer which connected the antiquated main building with a newer addition. The elevator only went up three floors, so Rob had to carry our three large suitcases and six smaller bags (after all, a woman has to do some shopping!) up a final flight of stairs with the assistance of a young Romanian porter who was working his first day on the job. The handsome, dark-haired youth with fine-chiselled features common to his fellow countrymen, commented: 'So many bags, Mister. You stay for long time, yes?'

'No, unfortunately, only two days,' Rob replied, which caused a ripple of laughter amongst us all.

After the long drive we needed to eat a light snack. As it was late, before even unpacking, we caught the elevator back to the lower-ground level, to a funny little restaurant with sleepy but friendly waiters, dressed in traditional brightly embroidered vests. As they spoke little or no English, Evelyn managed our orders since, despite both our fathers being born Romanian, their native tongue was Hungarian (like both their mothers) so the few basic words Rob and I knew were Hungarian. They were not helpful at all as it is not spoken in Timişoara regardless of its proximity to the border. There's a rivalry that exists between the Hungarians and Romanians through the centuries, because following several wars, the national borders have moved several times, leaving the city a hostage of one country or another.

We ordered a *Forte Bun* (Romanian for Farmer's Snack), which was *delishos*—a word we used often over the next few days. With every meal, even with breakfast which we ate in our funny little hotel, the welcoming waiters, for whom nothing was too much trouble, served the four of us with a shot of *Palinca*—a type of very strong fruit-flavoured liquor or schnapps. For me, even the smallest sip felt like receiving a strong whack in the face.

Several serendipitous or eerie events occurred during our far-too-short stay in our fathers' homeland. The first was when eating our *Forte Bun* on our late arrival at the Hotel Savoy, with just the four of us keeping our Romanian chef busy when the kitchen should have been closed. As we made plans for visiting Rob's dad's (Steven) childhood residence, and filling Evelyn in on her Uncle Steven's well-being, all of a sudden Steven's all-time favourite singer, Demis Roussous's, distinctive vocals could be heard softly in the background.

'Here's to Uncle Steven!' Evelyn said, as she downed a shot of *Palinca*.

Then, the following day before setting off in the car, I decided to take a stroll around the block as I had only just realised that the hotel was located very close to where my father (Fred) used to live. The hotel booking was made by our travel agent, and at the time of the booking I was still trying to locate the actual street name where Dad had lived as it didn't exist on any of today's maps. It had taken me several attempts, but fortunately, just before our departure from home, a diplomat from the Australian Embassy in Romania answered my enquiry, informing me that the majority of inner-city street names had been changed after the war when the new communist government took over. With Dad still able to recall not only his old street name and number, but also the closest adjoining side street, the embassy had given me detailed directions to where his home still stood, some 70 years after he and his family had fled. However, as fortunate as it was to be staying just a six-minute walk from that street (or *Strada*), what I didn't realise until after that first walk, was that when I drew back the curtains from our fourth-floor hotel room, I could actually see the roof top of my father's home.

Being so close, we walked there a few times. And each time I stood outside the large wrought-iron fence and gates, admiring the well-kept two-storey townhouse (almost exactly as Dad had described it), I could imagine Dad playing soccer on the very same cobblestone street, my grandmother calling him inside from the balcony window, and all the other lullabies she had shared with me as she taught me to cook some of her, and now my family's, favourite recipes. And as I walked in my ancestors' footsteps, I felt a stirring sensation—as if my grandmother, Anyu, was holding my hand, saying: 'Welcome Cherie-ka. What has taken you so long to visit me?'

Evelyn drove us the ten or so kilometres to the outer-city suburb of Chisoda, where Rob's father used to reside. Rob recalled different landmarks from his only other visit with his family in 1974, when he was 19 years old—the year before we met each other.

'Nothing has changed in 40 years,' he kept saying, as we passed some very rundown buildings and eyesores—including a large gas pipe running above ground for many kilometres down the sides of some of the main streets, even up and over intersections and crossroads, rusty and full of holes.

Chisoda itself was pretty and quiet with small stone or brick houses painted in a muted Tuscan-coloured canvas. Roses were blossoming in well cared for gardens and, with vivacious children playing in the streets, the suburb felt it had more life in its small houses than the earlier grey, airless inner suburbs of Timişoara.

We visited Evelyn's family home which was located just a few houses away from Steven's family home. Evelyn's father, Ludwig, had built it by hand, including an underground cellar for the distilling of wine and *Palinca*, as well as the brewing of beer. Even though we couldn't get inside the high fence, as we peered over, Rob recalled that during his visit in 1974, he was asked to fetch some wine or beer for the adults and discovered a trapdoor which was partially hidden in the long grass. As cousins, Rob and Evelyn, felt very connected with each other and their surroundings, and even re-enacted a photo that I had used in *With Just One Suitcase,* in which Evelyn, Steven, some local children and their goat, had posed in 1974.

Then we visited their grandparents' and uncles' graves. It was a very emotional experience seeing them, the large joint tombstone of the grandparents inscribed with: 'Nicolaus and Katarina König'. They had passed away three years apart: 1967 and 1970. Since writing the book, I felt I knew them well. Naturally, we took lots of photos and, uncannily, when we looked at them later that night, we discovered that as Rob and Jon stood on either side of the grandparents' grave, from between the large trees behind it, the setting sun cast a glorious beam directly over them—the ray of light resembling a consecrated star, eerily illuminating the sacredness of the moment.

On our final day in Timişoara, we spent some time revisiting the city centre. The Opera House and Romanian Orthodox Cathedral dominate Victory Square, and in the middle of the garden piazza, I was fascinated to see the she-wolf statue that Dad had described as his favourite—a replica of the famous *Lupa Capitolina* in Rome. I also found the largest Jewish synagogue which, although closed now, I was sure Anyu and Apu would have attended.

As the time approached to bid our farewells to Evelyn, who was remaining behind with friends, we felt torn … we were leaving a large piece of ourselves in Timişoara. It had taken me 57 years to retrace my ancestors' footsteps and all at once I felt both sad to say goodbye yet happy at what I had discovered.

Along with the staff at the Savoy Hotel who had come to know us, we had our final toast of *Palinca* as they loaded our car with several plastic soft drink bottles of the stuff to take with us! We made a toast to Timişoara, to family, to the past *… as sometimes it's from yesterdays that we find our tomorrows.*

Located on the Buda side of the Danube, we arrived safely at our Art Deco style hotel shortly after 7 p.m. and set off on foot to find something for dinner. Being a Sunday evening, however, local restaurants were closed, so we ended up eating a burger from Burger King instead of the Hungarian feast we'd been dreaming of. To be honest, though, we were actually too exhausted to care. After the previous three days we were both emotionally and physically overcome, but at least it meant we slept like logs in our elaborately decorated hotel, with its large comfy beds.

Budapest was hazardous to drive around, but Rob somehow managed to get us to all the traditional landmarks with just a few horns tooting my last-minute navigation. *Szent Istvan's Basilica* (St Stephen's Basilica), named in honour of Hungary's first king, is the largest church in Hungary. Constructed in a neo-Renaissance design, its ornate interior of green and gold is spectacular. After taking it all in, lighting another candle and praying for the same miracle which I had done in all of the cathedrals and basilicas we had visited along the way, Jon and I made our way outside to the plaza.

The day was hot, and while we waited in the shade for Rob, who had gone missing in action, I began thinking about finding some *langos* (deep fried flat bread) for lunch.

'Hey, Chez,' Rob called excitedly, as he jogged up to us. 'You're not going to believe what just happened to me! I asked a security guard about Puskás' crypt, 'cos I'd heard it was underneath St Istvan's, and at first he said to me: "No, no … it is private, family only". So I told him I was a big fan of Puskás[4] and had travelled from Australia to visit. And guess what? He took me aside and whispered: "Okay, come with me". So, we go down a flight of stairs and he unlocks a door and ushers me in. And there it was … set in stone … He even took some pictures of me in front of the inscription: "The Private Crypt of Puskás".'

After that highlight, not far away we found a street stall selling *langos*. People were queued up ordering all sorts of toppings (a bit like a pizza stall). We ordered ours plain with just garlic and salt, devouring them in minutes. Delicious! Each bite triggered fond memories of Rob's dad cooking them by the hundred at every home game played by his beloved St George Budapest Soccer Team, where he—along

---

4. Ferenc Puskás (1927-2006) was a Hungarian footballer, widely regarded as one of the greatest footballers of all time. A prolific forward, he scored 84 goals in 85 international matches for Hungary, and 514 goals in 529 matches in the Hungarian and Spanish leagues. He was voted top goal scorer of the 20th century by IFFHS. He became an Olympic champion in 1952 and led his nation to the final of the 1954 World Cup where he was named the tournament's best player. He won three European Cups (1959, 1960, 1966), 10 national championships (5 Hungarian and 5 Spanish Primera División) and 8 top individual scoring honors.

with fellow migrant 'football' tragics from that era—worked tirelessly, bringing to life the halcyon days of the world game to Australia.

We spent the last three days of our five-week trip visiting all the interesting, beautiful and historical sights of Buda and Pest which combine to make a magnificent city renowned as the 'Paris of the East'. Budapest, more than any other city, is the queen of the Danube. It is literally built on the river, with several bridges, including the famous Chain, Elisabeth and Liberty Bridges, connecting Buda to Pest. The Houses of Parliament face the Danube, and at the rear is a plaque with bullet holes, commemorating the Hungarian Revolution of 1956—a nationwide revolt against the government of the Hungarian People's Republic and its Soviet-imposed policies. It lasted from 23 October 1956 until 10 November 1956 with over 2,500 Hungarians and 700 Soviet troops killed in the conflict. More than 200,000 Hungarians fled as refugees, many following in the footsteps of their post-World War II compatriots ... to the sanctuary of Australia.

What little we knew of Hungarian was put to good use as we made our way around, visiting distinctive landmarks such as the famous thermal springs' spa baths at The Gellert Hotel, and Buda Castle, from which we captured a splendid panoramic view of the city.

All too quickly, it was time to say *viszontlátásra* (see you again) to Budapest. Our flight back to Dubai took four and a half hours. I cried as the plane taxied out to depart; and as the wheels left the firmness of the runway and we became airborne, the disconnect from our roots tugged at my heartstrings.

19

Stubbornly glad

Despite a wondrous overseas holiday where I rediscovered a small piece of me that I had forgotten existed, within these four walls called home is where my true self dwells. Our wells of identity are encapsulated by the self-civilising activities that a house, or more accurately a home, enables. At home, the things I enjoy most—my writing, reading books in the sun, tending my roses, cooking for family, conversations with friends—are all accessible when needed. And I am surrounded by the ones I love most, including of course, my adorable granddaughters. My sense of spirit is animated and my desire to live long is ignited by their presence. Indeed, the best panacea for my ailments is found in the simplicity of just being with them.

Flashbacks to a time when my constitution was rendered bankrupt from aggressive chemo and radiation surreptitiously catch me off guard now and then. However, not being one to look back, I refuse to let the demons take up residence. There is, after all, too much to be thankful for. In all honesty, though, as my autoimmune diseases progressively confine me, I will admit my unseasoned mode, or I guess vulnerability, is to turn inward—everything I preach to others to avoid regarding social isolation and its pitfalls. So yes, sometimes I feel like giving up—feel the weight of being a burden on my family, especially Rob. But the thing is, *I won't*. Not now, not ever. I guess it isn't *in my blood*.

And so, I have allowed myself to find peace with all that has transpired. I know who I am: Cheryl Jane Koenig, besotted wife, fortunate mother and grateful grandmother. A human being made up of millions of finite cells as vulnerable as any other and still with much to learn. I am, however, *more than my illness*. I am less naive, less of a fool than I once was in ever believing that I am special. More humble, more subtle, more aware of how little I know. Less superior (I hope!), as I know I haven't got life all worked out.

Sometimes at night I am completely and utterly terrified, overwrought with pain, then I remember how blessed I am, and that when tomorrow comes, it will be a gift. After all, I might meet another inspirational carer or have another opportunity to speak publicly or attempt to gather my flittering thoughts into prose or, best of all, cuddle my granddaughters. My family are the reason I smile. They are my happy place, my frustration, what makes my heart beat and sometimes break.

Of course, there's the reality of all the rubbish stuff that happens to each of us, but life can still be full of laughter and adventures—only of a different sort for some, depending on the circumstance.

Indeed, no one has control over their every circumstance. And although we cannot always define our own destiny, I do believe, with the right attitude, it is possible to define our *quality* of life. After all, life is about choices, about resilience, about self-belief, about hard work. It's also about recognising your own limitations and apologising when you are wrong. I know I have foibles. My mistakes frequently whisper in my ears … many a word said that I wish could be taken back. Hopefully, my gaffes are lessening as I trek on. I am doing my best to be a better listener; to listen without the intent to judge but with the intent to understand, to empathise. There are many things said that do not require a comment or response. Commenting is often repeating what is already known. But listening with the intent to understand, that's when *I* learn.

On the flipside, I have stopped feeling a need to explain myself, or to pretend everything is okay, even when it's not, as I realise that most people only understand from their own perception. And what we perceive today is usually bootstrapped on previous opinion—with each of us viewing the past, and often the present, through a different lens.

Writing this memoir has been difficult. There have been long gaps in finding the mental agility or physical ability to get my fingers diligently to the keyboard. In fact, the manuscript lay dormant and unfinished for a few years, with me having the same thoughts or doubts I expressed in the author's note at the very beginning … I felt I was being egotistical to write at length about *myself.*

So, what changed? Well, sometimes it only takes a small word of encouragement to lift you back up on the path you belong. Not so long ago, during one of my annual medical examinations at the RPA with Professor Barnett and his neuro-immunology team (which includes a team of about four specialists) Dr Stephen Adelstein, a leading immunopathologist[1], always interested, always considerate

---

1. Immunology deals with the diagnosis and monitoring of diseases in which the immune system is underactive, such as immunodeficiencies that lead to susceptibility to infection and those in which it is overactive like autoimmune and allergic conditions. Source: Medicine is Pathology, www.rcpa.edu.au

in his patient care, happened to ask me what my next book would be about.

'Oh, I'm not sure,' I replied, a half-truth perhaps, but the same one I had given to so many others who enquired.

'Why don't you write about yourself? I think your attitude to life, your ability to function despite your chronic illness, would inspire a lot of people out there having a difficult time.'

And that was all that was necessary to enable me to put fingers to keys once more. It has been extremely rewarding, and I am most grateful for Dr Adelstein's kind words. Completing this memoir has helped me focus more on my fortunate life, for which I am *stubbornly glad*. Writing always teaches me something. And with this project I discovered there exists an important universal law of nature: for every reward in life there has to be an investment, whether time, money or hard work. I am, once more, a willing investor.

These days, though, I am very conscious of the fact that life is not as long as we think, that none of us can predict how long the sands will run in our hourglass. Conscious, too, that no one has a monopoly on suffering. And even though I am someone who now lives more carefully, with less abandon, I am also someone who thanks her lucky stars for every scratch and scar as they are reminders to live a more gracious and humble life.

With the quiet contentment of a woman who loves her family and is loved in return, I only hope I am deserving of all that I am blessed with.

For I enjoy life just as it is.

Postscript

On 4 August 2018, my past almost caught up with me, or I with it, following another serious medical episode.

As earlier described, over the last few years my pain levels from both the transverse myelitis and Sjogren's disease were testing me, to say the least. At my quarterly appointment with my sympathetic rheumatologist, a two-course infusion of an immune-suppressant drug called Rituximab (used for both cancer treatment and management of inflammatory diseases like rheumatoid arthritis, Lupus, Sjogren's disease and others) had been suggested as another, and in fact only, remaining drug that could possibly offer some reprieve.

After doing some research I discovered the common side effects from Rituximab sounded dreadful, let alone the uncommon side effects, for which, I laughingly suggested to the specialist, I was sure to be a candidate. So this, combined with the memory of how disgusting four months of chemotherapy made me feel some eight years ago, made me reluctant to go ahead; on two occasions I actually cancelled the scheduled infusions.

However, mid 2018, I had a routine appointment with my rheumatologist. He indicated that he had absolutely nothing left in his 'bag of tricks' to help me and reiterated that he believed Rituximab was worth a shot as not only could it help with my inflammatory pain, but also quite possibly with my debilitating gut problems. Reluctantly, I decided to pluck up the courage and give it a go.

'I just have to face the fact I will feel disgusting for a month or so, and cancel all my plans,' I said to Rob.

With that decision, appointments were made for the first two weeks in August.

Leaving home at 7 o'clock to tackle the peak-hour traffic, Rob, Jon and I arrived at the RPA on the chilly winter's morning of Thursday August 2, at 8.30 a.m. As directed, I had taken an antihistamine and paracetamol an hour before the infusion (to reduce the risk of the common side effects of breathing difficulty and fever). After completing the necessary paperwork, a catheter was inserted into my one good remaining vein, in my right arm (all others having given up the ghost years ago from the rigors of chemo), and I settled back into the unpretentious blue recliner chair as the infusion began.

Before long, a nurse noted that my blood pressure had dropped to 80 over 50.

'Don't worry,' I assured them, feeling fine, 'I have low blood pressure anyway. Normal for me is somewhere between 95 and 110.' But the nurse called the doctor and they decided to stop the infusion and give me a bag of saline to help pump my blood pressure back up. That seemed to do the trick, so after half an hour we recommenced the Rituximab.

A little later, Rob and Jon left to get themselves some lunch and bring me back a toasted sandwich. Shortly after that, my blood pressure was taken again, and it was on the low side once more. As I had no other symptoms—other than a bit of light-headedness—it was decided to forge ahead or we would never get it done in a day. Around 3 o'clock, with a little more than an hour of Rituximab to go, the nurse wasn't happy with my blood pressure again.

'You just don't want to go home tonight, do you?' she joked, as she tilted my reclining chair backwards to raise my legs higher than my head. 'Here, drink this bottle of water.'

We left after four, hitting afternoon traffic and didn't arrive home till around five-thirty.

'I feel fine,' I told Rob and whoever else telephoned to ask that evening, 'considering how I used to arrive home feeling from chemo in bygone days'.

The next morning, Rob made breakfast and I helped Jon dress for his Friday job at Slater and Gordon's Liverpool office. I was feeling a bit off —a tad dizzy with nausea setting in—but in my mind, nothing that should prevent Rob from going to work that afternoon.

As the nausea worsened and the diarrhoea began suddenly and severely, I realised I wouldn't be able to pick Jon up from work that afternoon, so I rang and organised a taxi to bring him home. After much of the afternoon spent in the bathroom, my body was beginning to ache all over, and around five, I recall thinking: *how the hell am I going to get Jon dinner with just the thought of food making me feel like vomiting?*

Fortunately, Danielle rang to see how I was faring. 'Not great,' I replied.

'I'm going to put the girls in the car and come and pick Jon up now. I'll take him home for dinner. And when Chris gets home around seven, he'll bring him home and help shower him.'

'No!' I feebly insisted. 'The last thing I want is for you to put your two little bubs in the car on this cold night and come out. We'll manage somehow.'

'You're always here for us; it's the least I can do. I'll be there in less than 15 minutes,' she insisted, and hung up.

Around eight, Chris and Jon arrived home. Looking back, all I can remember of how I spent those hours are of making mad dashes to the bathroom ... sometimes there in time, mostly not!

'With Dad working tomorrow, I'll be staying the night,' Chris said firmly as he saw me to bed.

'No, Chris. I'll be fine in the morning. I'd rather you just go home and be with your girls. They hardly get to see you through the week. Weekends are precious to you all.'

'I've already brought my things from home. I'll stay and get Jon and you breakfast and help Jon dress, then I'll go home after that.' I knew by his tone not to even try to negotiate. Chris, now 31, was a well-liked and respected senior engineer at the same engineering consultancy company he had completed his internship with in his final year of university. He led a true and dignified life, always attentive, always everything to everybody. He stayed the night, leaving around nine the next morning, shortly before Jon was picked up by a carer attendant for his regular Saturday activities: an hour at the gym, followed by lunch and a movie.

After they had both gone, the continuing diarrhoea, nausea and muscle aches made me feel weary, so I lay down on my bed, drifting in and out of sleep which was more like some weird hallucination from which I couldn't wake up.

Only when my mobile rang, was I was able to wake myself up sufficiently to answer.

'Chez, you sound terrible. What's happening?'

'Thank God, you rang, because I couldn't wake myself up from this nightmare-like state. I've got to get up. I need to have something to drink and try and eat some crackers or something,' I replied.

After hanging up, I went downstairs and sat at the kitchen table sipping some water and nibbling dry crackers. All of a sudden, my body started to tremble. Within seconds the tremble turned to violent shaking. 'What the hell is going on?' I said out loud. But then I got up and had trouble walking. So, thinking I needed to go back to bed to let whatever was happening run its course, I carefully made my way to the staircase. By some stroke of good fortune or (or judicious thinking), without understanding what was happening to me, but realising it wasn't good, I had the presence of mind to unlock the front door before crawling up the staircase on hands and knees. I climbed onto my bed with the thought that I'd wait it out. *Surely this fierce shaking can't last more than a few more minutes.*

How long did I lie there? Not sure.

Maybe 15 minutes, maybe even closer to half an hour later, as I literally clung to the bedclothes to stop myself from shaking sideways off the bed, I realised I needed help. I got my mobile phone out of my pocket. I tried to ring Chris, but my hands were shaking so violently, I couldn't hit the shortcut on my home screen. 'Concentrate,' I told myself as my fingers wobbled cruelly left and right of the small picture of his face. After several failed attempts, with a sudden stroke of good luck, somehow, I managed to touch the right place on the screen. He answered straight away.

'Chris…I…need…help,' my voice quavered.

'I'm coming, Mum. I'll be there in five minutes.'

We had only just finished renovations to our 34-year-old home, and had changed all the door handles, including the front door lock so Chris had not yet been updated with a new key. Unlocking the front door before I climbed the stairs played a huge part in saving my life that day, as did Chris, who within minutes of our phone call ending, I heard running up the stairs calling, 'Mum? Mum!'

By this time I knew I was in a really bad state. The violent shaking hadn't let up at all and was taking its toll, making my body hurt all over, with a major headache taking hold.

'I…need…an…ambulance…Chris.'

'You need to speak to them so you can tell them what drug you've had and what's happened since. Can you do that, Mum?'

'O…kay.'

Afterwards, when Chris finished off the conversation and placed the house phone back on its receiver, he said they told him the nearest ambulance was at least twenty minutes away.

'Chris…my…head…is…throbbing.' I closed my eyes and rubbed my forehead. Soon the darkness before my veiled lids turned to milky white and I began drifting through what looked like a long white square corridor. *What the hell am I doing in here?* I said to myself. *Good Lord, this is not good. I need to get out of this place!*

So I mustered every ounce of strength and forced myself to listen for Chris's voice, which sounded very distant but reassuring.

'Just breathe Mum,' he was saying. 'Slow your breathing down and focus on taking deep breaths.' And then I could feel his hands on my legs rubbing them, trying his best to alleviate the shaking.

'My…head… hurts…Chris.'

'Just hang in there, Mum. The ambulance will be here in a few more minutes.'

Suddenly there were two blurry figures in dark clothing leaning over me, one taking my temperature. A female voice: 'Temp's over forty. Heart rate 150'.

Another female voice began asking me questions. I knew I had to listen, to focus, to stay present. I did my best to answer and I remember one telling me that despite being in septic shock[1], my mental capacity was still fine, which was a positive sign. They gave me something for pain and fever (I presume) and some minutes later asked if I was able to walk down the stairs with their assistance. I said, yes, and despite feeling like I was walking on a thick sponge, slowly made it to the ambulance parked in our driveway.

As they settled me down and strapped me in, I saw Chris peering into the ambulance with an anxious look.

'Thanks, Chrissy. Don't worry, okay?' I said weakly. 'Can you try ringing Dad again,' I added as they the ambulance door slid closed.

Understanding that my complete medical history was at the RPA, the kind paramedics broke their protocol of taking patients to the nearest hospital, and took me all the way to the

---

1. Septic shock is when you experience a significant drop in blood pressure that can lead to respiratory or heart failure, stroke, failure of other organs, and death.

RPA (an hour's drive from our home) as they rightly thought that would be in my best interest. Chris followed in his car.

About half an hour into the trip, my intense shaking finally stopped. 'Thank goodness for small mercies,' I said. But my mind was really elsewhere. I thought only of Rob and Jon—how would they know where to find me? What would Jon's carer attendant do with him? I was still scared—I knew septic shock was a serious condition.

I needed Rob. I needed my soulmate's hand in mine.

Of course, I needn't have worried. Chris had it all under control. As the ambulance arrived at Emergency and they were sliding my gurney out the rear doors, I heard Rob's familiar whistle. A few seconds later he was calling out, 'Chez! Chez! I'm here.'

'Oh, Rob,' I said, relieved, as he appeared next to me. 'Chris was trying to get you for ages. Your damn phone still doesn't work properly at the airport!'

'I'm here now,' he said, taking my hand and kissing it, as they wheeled me through corridors and into the ED. 'And don't worry about Jon. Chris has organised Zoe to take him back to Mum and Dad's.'

I stayed in the high dependency unit of the ED for the next eight hours or so. Every time they tried to move me into the normal part of their casualty department to wait for transfer to a ward, my blood pressure and other vital signs continued to play havoc.

After several hours, later that night, I was eventually transferred to the Intensive Care Unit (ICU), and it was here I stayed for the next five days. During that time I was fed multiple types of antibiotics, ongoing meds to raise my blood pressure which was continuing to prove tricky to keep above 85—sometimes dropping as low as 60-something, continuous saline through another catheter, very high doses of steroids, plus various other nutrients that the diarrhoea had presumably wiped out. As well as dangerously low blood pressure, now my heart rate was hazardously low. I still had the diarrhoea, but I couldn't produce urine, so a catheter was inserted into my bladder. On day two, an arterial line was cut into my wrist and another catheter inserted into an artery and then stitched in place, which would hopefully allow the drugs to have a better effect.

It was also on day two that I noticed my feet and ankles were puffy and swollen. Before long they were like tree stumps. My hands also swelled up and I was unable to get my rings off—even for an MRI scan. Sometime later, Rob told me I didn't look like myself as my face had become puffy with fluid as well. All this, I later learned, are signs of organ failure, which also showed up on my MRI with 'bilateral pleural effusion'[2].

After three tiring days and sleepless nights in ICU, I asked one of the kind nurses providing me with one-on-one 24-hour care, why it was necessary for me to waste what was surely a very much in-demand ICU bed.

---

2. Pleural effusion is a build-up of fluid in the pleural space, an area between the layers of tissue that line the lungs and the chest cavity. It may also be referred to as effusion or pulmonary effusion. Causes of pleural effusions include congestive heart failure (the most common cause overall) https://www.medicinenet.com/pleural_effusion_fluid_in_the_chest_or.../article.htm

'Cheryl,' she replied, 'I don't think you realise how sick you are. Even with vasopressors[3] we can't get your blood pressure up. See your reading on the monitor in brackets after your blood pressure?'

'Yes.'

'That's your MAP[4]—mean average pressure. We'd like it to be around 65, and yours is in the 50s. Your heart rate is now too low and your core body temp is just over 35 degrees. Just because your blood cultures have come back negative for bacterial infection, doesn't mean you weren't in septic shock. You had all the clinical signs of it.'

'Oh, right. What's the difference between sepsis and septic shock?'

'Virtually the same thing. Sepsis is usually caused by an infection that triggers a high fever, weakness, rapid heart rate, and rapid breathing. It can affect internal organs such as the kidneys, heart and lungs, which can fail if not treated. Septic shock is when the sepsis causes dangerously low blood

---

3. Vasopressors are agents that cause constriction of blood vessels, leading to an increase in blood pressure. Some vasopressors are also positive inotropes (capable of increasing contractility of the heart) and/or positive chronotropes (capable of increasing heart rate). Vasopressors are commonly administered intravenously in the critical care setting to treat conditions such as severe hypotension and cardiac arrest. Appropriate treatment of sepsis includes prompt identification, early antimicrobial drug therapy, appropriate fluid resuscitation, and initiation of vasopressors in the presence of continued septic shock. http://ccn.aacnjournals.org/content/23/4/79.long\ https://www.ncbi.nlm.nih.gov/pubmed/29336676

4. The mean arterial pressure (MAP) is calculated by the formula: where DBP and SBP are diastolic and systolic blood pressure, respectively. Mean arterial pressure is a useful concept because it can be used to calculate overall blood flow, and thus delivery of nutrients to the various organs. https://www.ncbi.nlm.nih.gov/books/NBK268/

pressure—which you've still got—sending the body into shock. That's why it's called "septic shock". And from this state, internal organs typically receive too little blood, causing them to fail. If not treated early, septic shock is life threatening. It was lucky your son came so promptly, because you could have lapsed into a coma.'

'Oh, my Lord, I knew it was bad, but not *that* bad!'

'We can't test for every bacteria,' she continued matter-of-factly as she went about taking my temperature and administering drugs, 'and you did come back positive for rhinovirus— the common cold—although you have no symptoms. Viral infection[5] is another cause of sepsis. But also, there's medical evidence suggesting you can go into septic shock from a severe adverse drug reaction. Do you know the mortality rate?'

'No idea.'

'Well, it is, in fact, one of the leading causes of death in the ICU. So you'll be here for as long as necessary.'

'Oh…' was all I could find to say again.

I didn't worry Rob with what the nurse had said, nor my other dear family and friends who visited. Esther, my longest and dearest friend, came often, bringing me love and support as she always has with every crisis. She was going through her own medical issues, and I was not about to add to her stress.

---

5. Sepsis and septic shock can result from an infection anywhere in the body, such as pneumonia, influenza, or urinary tract infections. While bacterial infections are the most common cause of sepsis, viral infections can cause sepsis too. Worldwide, one-third of people who develop sepsis die. Many who do survive are left with life-changing effects, such as post-traumatic stress disorder (PTSD), chronic pain and fatigue, organ dysfunction (organs don't work properly) and/or amputations. https://www.sepsis.org/ sepsis-and/viral-infections/

It was not until day five that they finally transferred me to a ward. My MAP was still low, but the doctors decided they needed to lower their expectations since my blood pressure was normally on the low side.

Another sleepless night was spent in a four-bed room. Three males occupied the other beds—one of whom had MRSA[6], another who had influenza and coughed continuously, and the third who sang country and western songs all night long (mind you, not accompanied by any pleasant music, just him singing and clicking his fingers). As soon as a doctor appeared the following morning, I said I wanted to go home where I could at least get a good night's sleep. The doctor agreed to my request but insisted I come back immediately if I deteriorated at all.

By the time all the paperwork was completed, it was late afternoon when Rob walked me to the car parked directly outside the front door of the hospital. I felt weaker than anticipated and had to recline the front seat just to stop my head from lolling about. Arriving home, it was dark and cold. I went straight to bed without any dinner and fell asleep soon after, but unfortunately, woke around midnight and couldn't fall back to sleep again. This would be the state of play for the next week or so, as I weaned myself from the high doses of steroids and other medications.

---

6. MRSA is the abbreviation for methicillin-resistant Staphylococcus aureus. Staphylococcus is a group of bacteria, familiarly known as Staph (pronounced "staff"), that can cause a multitude of diseases as a result of infection of various tissues of the body. https://www.emedicinehealth.com/mrsa_infection/article_em.htm

One night, during that first week at home, I told Rob about what the nurse had said—how she had confirmed the paramedic's quick diagnosis of my condition as sepsis or septic shock, which, despite my attempts of keeping calm and not wanting to alarm Chris, had startled me greatly at the time.

'You know the worst part of that day,' I said to Rob as he lay next to me on the bed, 'was the thought that I might not get to say goodbye to you'. My voice started to quiver and tears rolled down my cheek.

'Don't upset yourself, Chez.'

'No, I've just got to say this to you now. When I was so scared that day, you were the one face, the one person, I needed to see most of all. I needed to tell you how much I love you—which I don't say often enough—and I desperately needed to thank you for everything you do for me. You know you're my very breath?'

'Thanks, Chez.' He said kissing me softly.

'But Rob,' I continued, 'it was the thought of never seeing you again, never hearing your voice again, that was so, so awful. I was just so relieved when I heard your whistle and then you calling my name, outside the hospital.'

'I'm always going to be by your side, darling. Now no more talk of dying, okay?'

'Okay, then. I promise I'll never die. You'll have me and my troubles forever and ever.'

'It's a deal, Lazarus!'

In Memoriam

In memory of all those brave souls whose battle with the big 'C' was lost despite every ounce of will and courage.

Kate Needham, who after steering me through my early alarming diagnosis which unquestionably contributed to my outcome, sadly lost her own brave battle with brain cancer in 2016. She was an inspirational lady of the highest calibre who will be remembered with tremendous admiration and gratitude.

Anthony Solylo, Rob's first cousin. With only two month's difference in age, they grew up as close as brothers. Tony was a treasured member of our extended family who made our large clan gatherings full of fun. A life over too soon from bowel cancer. Always loved, never, ever forgotten.

Michael (Mick) Meehan, who, for 30-plus years was our family plumber and good friend. Stage-four kidney cancer took this strong, always cheerful man, in only four short months from diagnosis.

Alex Pongrass AM, one of Australia's most successful post-World War II entrepreneurs whose remarkable life story sadly came to a close in June 2000. Arguably, in the post-war era there were very few men with his dynamic charisma, vision for both business and sport, and calibre for creating new and successful ventures with innate intuition and an extraordinary work ethic. His passing, from stomach cancer, was significant—not only for his family and close friends—but for many thousands of people whose life paths had the good fortune to cross with his.

And far too many others ...